INQUISITION

INQUISITION

JOHN EDWARDS

TEMPUS

First published 1999
This edition first published 2003

Tempus Publishing Limited
The Mill, Brimscombe Port,
Stroud, Gloucestershire, GL5 2QG
www.tempus-publishing.com

British Library Cataloguing in Publication Data.
A catalogue record for this book is available from the British Library.

ISBN 0 7524 2857 8

Typesetting and origination by Tempus Publishing Limited
Printed in Great Britain by Midway Colour Print, Wiltshire

CONTENTS

A map showing the tribunals of the Inquisition. Names in italics indicate tribunals dependent on the Council's secretariat for Aragon; the rest were dependent on the secretariat for Castile.

ACKNOWLEDGEMENTS

Many individuals and groups have contributed to the possibility of completing this work. They include academic
colleagues, too numerous to mention by name, in Britain,
Spain, Israel, France, the United States and elsewhere. They
may not agree with everything, or indeed anything, written
here, but they have all contributed in greater or lesser ways to
the outcome. This short book is also offered, with gratitude,
to the students and staff with whom I worked, over a period
of twenty years, in the University of Birmingham, and in
particular to those who followed my courses on Jewish
history between the First Crusade and the Counter-
Reformation, and on Christian heresy and the beginnings of
the Inquisition, between 1200 and 1350. I am also grateful for
the insights provided by the staff members and students of the
former Centre for the Study of Judaism and Jewish-Christian
Relations, and of the fortunately still active Centre for the
Study of Islam, in the Selly Oak Colleges, Birmingham, as
well as the past and present officers and members of the
Council of Christians and Jews, both in Britain and interna-
tionally. I further acknowledge the insights and (generally

constructive) provocation of those with whom I have worshipped over many years, in All Saints' Church, King's Heath, and St Alban and St Patrick, Highgate, in Birmingham, as well as the ecumenical chaplaincy of St Francis' Hall, in the University of Birmingham. I also owe a special debt to the city of Córdoba, and acknowledge the unique inspiration of its rich, and sometimes violent, history of the relationships between Christians, Jews and Muslims.

In the production of this book, I am especially grateful to my publisher, Jonathan Reeve, for his initial commission and continuing enthusiasm and encouragement, and to Kate Adams for her work in bringing the text and illustrations into production. A number of illustrations have been provided by my wife Vivien, who is a comparatively recent convert to the love of Spain. I also gratefully acknowledge the help, kindness and hard work of Elena de Santiago, head of the Service of Drawings and Engravings of the Spanish National Library in Madrid, in securing items from the library to illustrate this book, and to the Library's Service of Reproductions for providing the necessary photographic materials. I am also grateful for the help of the director of the Sephardic Museum at Toledo, Ana María López Álvarez, and her staff, in providing illustrations of items in the museum and of the Synagogue of 'El Tránsito', which is its home, and to Messrs Foto Arte San José, Toledo, for their photographic work.

I also warmly thank the Perpetual Secretary of the Royal Academy of History in Madrid, Eloy Benito Ruano, and José Manuel Andrade, for their efforts and kindness in securing transparencies from the Prado Museum and the Museum of the Royal Academy of Fine Arts of San Fernando, both in Madrid. I thank all these institutions for their co-operation.

Finally, I am grateful to the George Bell Institute, at the Queen's College, Birmingham, and in particular its director, Andrew Chandler, for a grant in aid of costs incurred illustrating this book.

Ioan van Hertz, showing perhaps the influence of William Blake, portrays a stylised image of torture by the Inquisition.

INTRODUCTION

In July 1986 a large group of Jews, Christians, Muslims and
Druze met in Spain for a conference, under the auspices of
the International Council of Christians and Jews. The main
sessions were held in the Pontifical University of Salamanca,
and, this being a Catholic place of learning, crucifixes were
prominently displayed on the walls of the lecture halls. While
the conference largely consisted of talks and dialogue,
separate worship was arranged for the various faiths, and in
addition joint sessions of prayer were planned. Some Jewish
delegates expressed the firm view, however, that they could
not pray in the presence of a representation of the crucified
Jesus, adding that this would be especially difficult for them
in Spain. The university authorities were unable to remove
the offending articles because they were embedded in the
walls, and the joint prayer sessions duly proceeded.

It could be argued that this incident encapsulates the
attitudes and emotions which arose in past centuries, and
which still arise from the often violent interaction between
Jews, Christians and Muslims in Spain – in particular, genuine
Jewish fear and apparent Catholic inflexibility, the latter

having been very real in past times. The Council of Christians and Jews itself began work in its present form in 1942, when the realisation had dawned, at least on some, that the real policy of Adolf Hitler, as ruler of the Third Reich, was not just to deport Jews but to wipe them and their religion from the face of the earth. Having started in Britain, the organisation spread around the world, and now has its headquarters in Heppenheim, Germany. Since 1945 various attempts have been made by different branches of the Christian Church to examine and confront those things in their past which have encouraged contempt for Jews and Judaism. In this climate, which has still had all too little influence on the day-to-day life of Christian congregations, although most secular interests are ready enough to see anti-Semitism as a gross abuse of universal human rights, it is not always thought to be desirable to stress the atrocities to which Jews, Muslims and others have been subjected in the past. The Inquisition, in Spain and elsewhere, makes a confrontation with the past unavoidable.

Not every page, let alone every paragraph, of what follows will contain direct denunciation of the Spanish Inquisition and its works. Yet the continuing need in Spain, as elsewhere, to discuss the so-called 'Black Legend' (*Leyenda negra*) indicates that the cruelties which were committed by the inquisitors and their officials against their fellow citizens are not forgotten, and are deemed by most to be unacceptable. Nevertheless, it would not be true to participants in the events of previous centuries to judge them simply and unquestioningly by the criteria of the departing twentieth century, which has in many cases set new standards of human depravity and hypocrisy. An effort will thus be made here to set the tribunals of the Spanish Inquisition in their proper historical context, including the religious presuppositions on which they based their activities. Although it is primarily set in Spain itself, this treatment of the Spanish 'Holy Office' of the Inquisition will also recognise the tribunals' links with Portugal, with other parts of Europe, and with some of the outposts of the Spanish and Portuguese empires. Every inquisitor claimed to be primarily interested in a happy outcome for those whom he investigated, even if the violence with which this was frequently attempted makes the claim seem highly implausible in many cases. If only a proper balance could be achieved, at the second millennium of the birth of Jesus, between the deep conviction which is necessary to sustain good human conduct, and tolerance of those who approach this goal by other means.

Oxford, 21 May 1999

I

BEFORE
THE INQUISITION

As for a man who is factious, after admonishing him
once or twice, have nothing more to do with him.
(Titus 3:10, Revised Standard Version)

[Jesus said] If a man does not abide in me, he is cast forth
as a branch and withers; and the branches are gathered,
thrown into the fire and burned. (John 15:6)

'Heresy', as commonly understood, is a purely Christian
concept. It is not to be found in the Jewish Scriptures which
preceded the collection of writings eventually designated by
the Church as the New Testament. Although the Biblical
records suggest that religious dissidence was frequently
condemned and punished by Jewish priests and prophets, it is
certain that there was considerable diversity of religious
opinion among the Jews of Jesus's and Paul's day. The original
Greek meaning of heresy, in pre-Christian times, was 'choice'
or a 'thing chosen', and it was commonly applied to the
support of a particular philosophical school and its tenets. In
the New Testament Epistle to Titus, which is traditionally

ascribed, as it was in the Middle Ages, to Paul the Apostle, the word *hairetikos* makes its sole appearance in the Bible. As well as a 'factious man', it can also mean a 'separatist'. The cognate noun *hairesis*, on the other hand, is used on a number of occasions in the New Testament in the sense of a religious party, such as the Sadducees and Pharisees in the Jewish Temple at Jerusalem (Acts 5:17 and 15:5), or indeed the 'sect' of the early Christians themselves (Acts 24:5). Both in the Acts of the Apostles, which were traditionally ascribed to Luke the Evangelist, and in Paul's first Epistle to the Corinthians, heresy was associated with partisan and dissident cliques (1 Cor. 11:19), and with the implication that false doctrine was leading to splits in the nascent Christian Church. The word had not yet acquired its medieval and later meaning of theological error, but it was soon to do so. The eventually martyred bishop of Antioch, Ignatius (*c.* AD 35–107), already used the term in this way, for example in his letter to the Ephesians (6:2). The early second-century text, which was included in the selection which became known from around AD 400 as the canon (meaning a rod or ethical norm) of New Testament Scripture as the 'Second Epistle of Peter', used the concept of heresy in the manner that would become familiar in the Middle Ages and later. 'But false prophets also arose among the people just as there will be false teachers among you, who will secretly bring in destructive heresies' (2 Pet. 2:1).

In the first few centuries of the history of the Christian Church, before the split between Catholic and Orthodox, the fear and rejection of heresy, in this sense of divisive and destructive teaching, played a major role in the formulation of orthodoxy. By the time of the Third Council of

Constantinople (680–1), the last of the seven 'Ecumenical Councils' (supposedly representing the whole inhabited world) which are still recognised as authentic by both Western and Eastern churches, a wide range of teachings about the nature of Christ and of His Church had been either adopted or rejected. It was on this doctrinal basis that the Catholic and Orthodox Churches expanded outwards from the Mediterranean basin during the late Roman and early medieval periods (*c*.400–1000). The pagan religions which the missionaries encountered, for example in the British Isles, Scandinavia, the Baltic regions and the Slav lands, were inevitably equated with the old internal enemy of heresy, which was to be fought by means of a mixture of orthodox doctrinal formulae and religious and secular repression. The mentality of 'Inquisition' had thus been established, but what were the antecedents of the Holy Office, which first arose in the western Catholic Church in the thirteenth century?

In the ancient world, there were miscellaneous heresies, rather than one undifferentiated mass known as heresy. The doctrinal edifice of the then still united Western and Eastern Churches had very largely been finished at the Ecumenical Council of Chalcedon, in 451. From then on, Christians were required to 'take it or leave it', rather than pick and mix in the supermarket of religious beliefs and practices. In the West, Augustine (354–430), who was bishop of Hippo, in North Africa, became for many the ultimate Christian doctrinal authority after the Bible and the Ecumenical Councils, yet his view of the nature of the Church has been often misunderstood since. Augustine thought that the Christian Church, despite its newly established canon of Scripture and doctrinal 'orthodoxy', was still nonetheless a community of sinners.

Although it already partook of the 'City of God', about which he famously wrote, the bishop of Hippo, who had once been a heretic himself in Catholic terms, believed that the Church was still rooted in the sinful earthly city ('carnal', or fleshly, in early Christian terminology). Later, though, his followers, who continue up to the present day in both Catholic and Protestant traditions, abandoned this qualification and asserted that the Church was indeed fully identified with the City of God. Thus every Christian dissident became a heretic, in the terms which had developed since the time of Ignatius of Antioch. From then on, the personal holiness of reforming Christians came up against the supposedly objective holiness of the Catholic Church. This added a potentially sinister aspect to the confusion which already existed in canonical Scripture between dissident views, or 'heresy', and dissident behaviour, or 'schism', the much-feared splitting of the Church. Another pointer to the future was that, even in Augustine's time, orthodox Catholics were appealing to the Imperial authorities, known in ecclesiastical jargon as the 'secular arm', to enforce the Church's authority against heretics.

Since the establishment and affirmation of Christian doctrine arose out of disputes with those who were eventually declared to be heretical, it can reasonably be argued that heresy is the inevitable result of the rationalisation of religion. The result of this deeply rooted notion of a pure and perfect Church, the conserver and protector of a divinely revealed orthodoxy, has been the establishment of two *idées fixes* about heresy, which seem to have survived the dissolution, in most Western people's minds, of any respect for the institution which caused them to come into being. The first of these ideas is that heresy, in accordance with the image of Jesus as the 'true Vine', which is developed in the fifteenth chapter of John's Gospel, is a dying branch on the tree-trunk of Catholicism. In the militaristic and chivalric imagery of feudal Europe, the metaphor might change to that of a dagger in the back, the act of the traitor. This view, which prevailed in the burgeoning science and practice of ecclesiastical or canon law (that Greek rod again!), presupposed that heresy originated within the body of Christ, the Church. Yet if the dead or infected branches were pruned, and burnt as dead wood, the orthodox tree would return, like that on which Jesus the Saviour was crucified, to life-giving health. The second conventional notion of heresy took an alternative view. In this account, using the medical imagery which played such a large part in medieval discourse on the subject, heresy was not an internal infection, or gangrene in the body, but a plague which attacked it from outside. Such an external enemy might be 'returned to sender', by means of expulsion, or else simply exterminated within Christendom itself. The effect of both these formulae was to excuse orthodox Catholics of all responsibility for faults within the Church, blaming them instead on enemies from within and without.

By the early eleventh century, the Western or Catholic Church, under the leadership of the Bishops of Rome as successors to the Apostle Peter, had effectively split from the Eastern Orthodox Churches. In secular terms, Western Europe was now ruled by a small number of kings and princes who, like contemporary popes, were struggling to develop their legal and bureaucratic authority over their subjects. Both popes and secular rulers were, however, faced with stout resistance from leading clerics, particularly bishops and cathedral canons, as well as from princes, nobles and knights. It was at this stage that heresy in the medieval Catholic Church, and its repression, began to be recorded. This point is important for any realistic appraisal of the nature and scale of Christian dissidence in the period before the foundation of the medieval Papal Inquisition. The eleventh and twelfth centuries were a time of growing literacy among ecclesiastical and secular bureaucracies, and this fact inevitably creates the danger of 'documentary illusion', which is a perennial danger for historians, in that it can lead to the lazy and unprovable assumption that phenomena do not exist unless someone writes them down. In the case of medieval heresy, the dangers of such an assumption are particularly acute, but the limited survival of written records inevitably means that modern knowledge of heretical belief and practice in the Catholic Church begins in the 1020s. At that time, Adhémar of Chabannes, a chronicler writing in Angoulême in western France, reported that in around 1022, ten canons of the cathedral at Orléans, 'who had seemed to be more religious than the others', were accused of being Manichaean heretics. King Robert I of France (reigned 996–1031) ordered them to return to the Catholic faith and, when they refused to do so, had them deprived of their priestly orders, expelled from the Church and burned to death. Adhémar accused the former canons of being Manichaeans, who had been led astray by a peasant who carried around the dust of dead children, and of worshipping the devil, who appeared to them either as an Ethiopian or as an angel of light. Groups of Manichaeans were said to have been active in much of southern France at this time, from Aquitaine to Provence. They were accused of holding beliefs similar to those of Mani (*c.*216–76), an Iranian who had made a 'dualistic' blend of Persian Zoroastrianism, Buddhism, Judaism and Christianity. In this system, which was to attract much attention from Church authorities in Western Europe between the eleventh and the fourteenth centuries, there were two rival creators: the good God, who made and ruled the heavenly, spiritual world, and Satan or the Devil, who created and controlled the material earth and its inhabitants. The Manichaean system involved the concept of reincarnation. In it, all material life, and in particular sexual reproduction, was regarded as totally sinful, and the souls of those who did not refrain from sex and lead a highly ascetic lifestyle would be trapped in a continuing cycle of rebirth into the Devil's kingdom. The only means of escape to the spiritual world was for a person to be baptized as a 'perfect one', or 'Cathar', and then live a completely sinless life until death.

It is highly questionable whether the ten unfortunate canons of Orléans had any such systematic beliefs. Throughout the period during which the medieval Inquisition developed, the normal practice of Church authorities was to identify any religious dissidence, however disorganised, in their own day with heresies of earlier periods. It is therefore hard to be sure that official accounts, which are generally the only sources available to the historian, are talking about contemporary events rather than the controversies of previous centuries. In any case, it appears that Adhémar is a far from disinterested source. At the time when he began to claim that the third-century heresy of Manichaeism was stalking the provinces of southern France, the chronicler was an embittered and disillusioned man. He had previously been at the forefront of the Catholic reform which was emerging from the Benedictine monasteries, and, in particular, had spent thirty years building up the cult of 'St' Martial of Limoges. This effort at reformed Catholic populism came to grief, however, when he was defeated in debate, in 1029, by a wandering monk called Bernard of Chiusa. After this, Adhémar seems to have seen heretics everywhere, and his case serves as a warning to those who take medieval accounts of heresy at face value. Nevertheless official efforts to repress religious dissidence continued throughout the eleventh century. The synod at Orléans, in 1022, which had burned at least the ten canons as a result of the so-called Manichaean movement, was the first known case of burnings for heresy in the medieval West. Two years later, Bishop Gerard of Arras summoned another synod to consider the cases of a group of suspected heretics, whom he had previously interrogated and released, but who were accused of having continued in their old beliefs. They seem to have been peasants, or possibly weavers, who aimed to abandon the working world in order to live entirely from their own resources and labour, and to give charity only within their brotherhood. This innocent faith did not save them from excommunication, and from having to mark with a cross a vernacular translation of a Latin version of the Catholic faith which had been placed before them. In 1028 or slightly later, a group of 'heretics' in the fortified village of Monforte, south of Turin, were examined by Archbishop Aribert of Milan, during a diocesan visitation. According to the only surviving source for the episode, the Milanese clerical chronicler Landulf, the group told the archbishop that they accepted the Old and New Testaments and canon law, as well as the authority of (unspecified) Church leaders.

They came into conflict with orthodoxy through their spokesman, Gerard, who stated that they prized virginity so highly that they disapproved of sex even within marriage, believing that without it, the human race would reproduce itself without coition, like the bees. It also emerged during the interrogation that the Monforte group rejected the authority of the Pope, in favour of an invisible spiritual authority, sent to them by God. They were taken to Milan, and attempts were made to convert them to orthodoxy, with success in some cases, though numerous of the unrepentant were burned.

Between 1050 and around 1100, while the programme of Church reform led by Pope Gregory VII was being implemented, and the Papacy in Rome was struggling against the German 'Holy Roman Empire' for control over the Western Church, there is little record of the identification and repression of heretical groups and individuals. This situation was to change, however, in the twelfth century, when a series of strong dissident thinkers appeared, to those in authority, to threaten the new and lovingly constructed edifice of the reformed, papal Church. The first of these figures, Henry, is known from either Le Mans in northern France or from Lausanne in Switzerland, where he was active. The sources which purport to describe Henry's errors are uniformly second-hand and hostile, but he appears to have been a lively and popular preacher, who gained a considerable following by denouncing the clerical estate, questioning the validity of priestly orders and increased clerical control over the administration of the sacraments of baptism and the Eucharist. He helped to bring about an uprising against the clergy of Le Mans, which succeeded in taking control of the city for

several weeks, beginning in Lent of 1116. He had been originally invited to preach in the town's cathedral, and the
diocesan bishop, Hildebert, had great difficulty in regaining
control when he returned from an Easter synod in Rome.
Excavation below the surface of the sources reveals that
Henry and his bishop were, despite appearances to the
contrary, in principle on the same side in their desire to
reform the Church. Henry seems to have been invited by
Hildebert to preach in the cathedral as part of the bishop's
campaign to reform its clergy and end abuses among the
priests of the rest of his diocese. Like numerous other Church
leaders of the period, Hildebert had adopted the high-risk
strategy of enlisting popular support for his aims from lay
Christians, who might be galvanised by rabble-rousing
preachers. In the case of Le Mans, Henry turned out to be
rather too radical for the bishop. He not only attacked clerical
greed and vice, but also asserted his own right to interpret the
Bible above that of the Fathers of the Church, such as
Augustine. He maintained that marriage was a private matter
for couples and not a sacrament of the Church, that
Christians should be baptised as adults and not as infants, and
that confession of sins should be made in public before the
whole congregation and not in private in the presence of a
priest. In other words, he saw the Church not as the hierarchical and perfected City of God, with its earthly leader, the
Pope, as Vicar of Christ, but as a body consisting of small and
largely independent groups of men and women. Although
Henry was eventually arrested, and interrogated before Pope
Innocent II at the Council of Pisa in 1135, he escaped with
his life and freedom, and his influence was felt long after in
both France and Italy.

Tortures, supposedly in an Inquisition prison, according to Cavallerius (1584).

Perhaps Henry of Le Mans/Lausanne's most notorious contemporary as a preacher and religious radical was Peter of Bruys. In around 1112, Peter began preaching against the Church establishment, in the foothills of the Alps to the east of the river Rhône, and continued, latterly in a loose alliance with Henry, until he was burned to death by orthodox Catholics in 1131. The only source for Peter of Bruys' teachings is a treatise *Against the Petrobrusians*, by the great abbot of the reformed Benedictine abbey of Cluny in Burgundy, Peter the Venerable (1092/4–1156), who, in the period between 1131 and 1140, wrote and revised a treatise which attempted to refute his views. The work formed part of a triptych of books written against Christian heretics, Jews and Muslims. According to Peter the Venerable, his opponent, whose influence had spread through much of southern France by the end of the 1120s, had similar views to those of Henry of Le Mans/Lausanne, but apparently took them to even greater extremes. Peter of Bruys is said to have rejected infant baptism, on the grounds that a Christian can only be saved by faith, and that a young child was not sufficiently aware of the world to be a believer. He rejected the use of consecrated churches, on the grounds that the Church consists of people, not stones. He held that the Cross should not be an object of veneration, but should rather be detested, because it had been used as an instrument of torture and degradation against Jesus. In accordance with this view, he and his followers were apparently in the habit of removing crosses and crucifixes from churches and burning them, especially on Easter Sunday, though this practice eventually led to his own demise when he was thrown by the Catholic faithful onto one of his own bonfires. He rejected the Catholic interpretation of the Eucharist, or Mass, on the ground that Christ's body and blood were consumed only once, at the Last Supper, on the eve of Jesus's betrayal by Judas, and that his sacrifice could not in any way be re-enacted. He repudiated the notion that prayers, Masses and offerings for the dead could in any way affect the fate of human souls, and he advocated the removal of plainsong from the liturgy, or services of the Church, in favour of silence and interior prayer.

Perhaps inevitably, given its blatant one-sidedness, Peter the Venerable's text reveals more of the Catholic authorities' approach to heresy than it does of the heresy itself. The issue here is not 'literacy' as such, that is, the ability to read and understand Latin texts, or even vernacular translations, but the intellectual and debating procedures which Peter deployed against his namesake Peter of Bruys, and his followers. Before the Inquisition was set up in the thirteenth century, heresy and schism were dealt with by means of a system of 'spiritual justice' which dated back at least to the fourth century, and which included the complete ecclesiastical condemnation known as anathema, excommunication, and ritual curses or comminations. In the tenth and eleventh centuries, these Church procedures became more complex, to match the development of arbitration procedures in the secular world. At the same time, the violence of the language used by papal supporters against the German emperors' attempts to control the Church spilled over into the treatment of humbler dissidents within it. In addition, Peter the Venerable's treatise against Peter of Bruys and his supporters reveals a new influence on the treatment of heretics in the twelfth century, which arose from the development of the cathedral schools and nascent universities, particularly in France and Italy. The Cluniac monk and heresy-hunter, on the basis of Paul's statement in I Corinthians 11:19, brought the debating skills of the schools to bear on what he held to be the inevitable need to purge heresy from the Church, which is the Body of Christ. This *purgatio* involved four stages, which deeply influenced subsequent inquisitorial procedures: *investigatio* (investigation), *discussio* (discussion), *inventio* (discovery), and *defensio* (defence). Thus the 'treatment' of the 'infection' of heresy in the Body of Christ, the Church, began with an inquest, or inquisition, which before the establishment of specialised tribunals was carried out by bishops or their representatives. The assembly of evidence from witnesses was followed by a debate between orthodox and heretical ideas which, in accordance with the current practice in the lecture halls of the new universities, were to be reduced to rational propositions, to be defended and attacked with all the rhetorical skills which were, at that time, being rediscovered and renewed in educated Church and secular circles. As the twelfth century came to an end, theological and intellectual techniques were in place to confront the 'threat' of heresy. The judicial apparatus of Church and state would soon be added, to create the Inquisition.

2

THE MEDIEVAL
INQUISITION

In the year 1170, according to one thirteenth-century account (or 1173 according to another), an inhabitant of the southern French city of Lyon, who is known to history as 'Peter' Valdes, or Waldo, seems to have had a drastic conversion. Modern scholars tend to assume that he was a merchant, and one of the sources, the town chronicle of the northern French city of Laon, describes him by what was then, in reforming Church circles, the highly abusive term of 'usurer'. There is no solid evidence for any of this, however, and the two main sources do not agree about the circumstances of the 'conversion'. The anonymous chronicler of Laon, who may have been an English monk and kept annals up to the year 1220, states that Valdes decided to change his lifestyle after hearing a travelling minstrel tell the story of St Alexis. According to the legends of the time, Alexis was the son of a Roman nobleman, who abandoned his wife on his wedding night to go on a lengthy pilgrimage. He eventually returned to Rome, and lived anonymously for seventeen years as a beggar outside his father's house, being identified after death by his handwriting, and, having become the source of miracles, was sanctified by the pope. In the account of the later chronicler, Stephen of Bourbon (*c.*1200–61), who was a member of the Dominican order in Lyon and wrote between around 1250 and 1261, Valdes reacted as he did after hearing a Gospel reading. Both sources state that the 'convert' sought guidance at once from the cathedral canons, either for his own personal salvation or else in order to obtain translations of the Latin Bible into French. As a result, he decided to abandon his former wealth and live a life based on the poverty of Jesus and his disciples. According to the Laon account, he returned home to offer his wife the unpalatable choice of either his movable or his immovable property, while his daughters were to be placed in a nunnery of the reformed monastic order of Fontevraud, which had been founded in 1100 by Robert of Arbrissel, for both men and women. His wife chose the real estate, while his money and other movable assets were divided between those whom he felt that he had wronged in his business life, and the poor, to whom he proceeded to distribute alms on a weekly basis, showing an example to his former friends by begging for his own food. After his wife had, not unreasonably, complained about her treatment to Archbishop Guichard de Pontigny, Valdes agreed at least to take his meals with her.

In 1179, two Valdensians, one of them possibly Valdes himself, went to Rome during the Third Lateran Council, in the St John Lateran palace in Rome, and presented to Pope Alexander III a French translation of various books of Scripture with glosses, or commentaries, and asked for the pope's authorisation to preach. In a session parallel to the Council, they were examined by Walter Map, a churchman who was a courtier of Henry II of England and chancellor of the diocese of Lincoln. Much to his own amusement, Walter claimed to have trapped them, in a form of university debate to which they were clearly not accustomed, into suggesting that they believed the Virgin Mary to be on a par with the Trinity of God the Father, Son, and Holy Spirit. Nevertheless, Alexander III apparently authorised these lay brethren to preach, provided that they were licensed by the Ordinary, or cleric in authority over them, in this case their archbishop. According to his own account, although Walter Map despised the Valdensians in front of him as 'simple and illiterate', he nonetheless feared that, if their understanding of the Gospel and its practice should prevail, his own kind, that is clergy who had higher education from which the great majority of Christians were excluded, would lose their pre-eminence. A year later, Valdes appeared before a synod in Lyon, and was interrogated by the papal legate, Henry of Marcy, Archbishop Guichard of Lyon, and Geoffrey of Auxerre, abbot of Hautecombe, the last of whom wrote an account of the affair. Valdes appears to have made a confession, or formal statement drawn up by others, of the Catholic faith and to have suffered no condemnation or sanction for any act against the doctrine and order of the Roman Church. After Archbishop Guichard's death in 1182/3, however, the new archbishop, John Bellesmains, reversed his predecessor's policy by condemning Valdes and his disciples, and expelling them from the city and diocese. After this nothing more is heard of Valdes, and there is no further record of Valdensians in Lyon. However, at the Council of Verona in 1184, Pope Lucius III condemned the so-called 'Poor of Lyon' as heretics, to be pursued with all rigour by Church and secular authorities.

Traditionally, Valdes, or 'Peter' Waldo, has been regarded by historians of the Church as a successor to rebellious preachers such as Henry of Le Mans/Lausanne and Peter of Bruys in France, and Arnold of Brescia in Italy. With the benefit of hindsight, he has also been regarded as a precursor both of Francis of Assisi and of Martin Luther. It has recently been suggested by Michel Rubellin that, like Henry in Le Mans before him, Valdes was in fact a pawn of a reforming archbishop, Guichard of Lyon. In this analysis, Guichard used his supposedly 'simple' and 'spontaneous' adoption of a lifestyle of total poverty, and his demands for the Bible in French and permission for himself and his lay companions to preach, in order to pressurise the largely aristocratic canons or cathedral clergy of Lyon to abandon their considerable private wealth and instead live in a religious community in the Cathedral, very much like monks. If this is true, Valdes's case would certainly not have been the first in which enthusiasts among the lesser clergy and laity had been used to further the aims of reforming monks and bishops (and popes) among the upper echelons of the Church. In any case, Valdensianism had become by 1200 a permanent part of the life of the Church, which continues to this day. Around the time of Valdes's death, which was probably between 1205 and 1218, his movement, which was originally known as the 'Poor Men of Lyon', began to split. One group, the 'Poor Lombards', developed in northern Italy, in the area of Milan and Piacenza, while the original Lyon disciples themselves split in 1207. In the next year, some of them were led by an Aragonese, Durandus of Huesca, back into the Catholic Church, where Pope Innocent III allowed them to form a group of 'Catholic Poor', which some have seen as a prototype for the Franciscan Order. Valdensians were to be targeted by the new Papal Inquisition throughout the rest of the Middle Ages, in northern Italy, southern Germany, and the lands which were eventually to become the Swiss Confederation. Their successors, both there and in Provence and southern Italy, were to link up with the followers of Luther in the early sixteenth century. By this time, the Valdensians were clearly in schism from the Catholic Church, but their doctrinal divergence was much less obvious around the year 1200, when they began to be subjected to violent oppression by the authorities of Church and State.

The earliest sources for Valdes and his movement strongly indicate that their disagreement with the Church hierarchy, after they had ceased to serve a polemical purpose for Archbishop Guichard of Lyon, was in matters of discipline rather than doctrine, particularly unlicensed lay preaching and the possession of Scriptures in languages other than Latin. One of the earliest orthodox writers on Valdensianism was the distinguished poet, philosopher and theologian Alan of Lille (*c.*1128–1203), who wrote during this period a lengthy treatise against the heresies of his day, in particular Catharism and Valdensianism. In the conventional vocabulary and imagery of Catholic writing against dissidents, with extensive quotation from the Bible, Alan described Valdes and his followers as wolves in sheep's clothing. To him, they were slanderers of Church leaders, and hypocrites because they themselves often failed to live up to the high standards of behaviour which they preached. Yet although he claimed that they blasphemed against God by means of 'heresy', he mentions no specific false theological doctrine which they held, and mainly attacks them for their ignorance and disobedience. Writing in the mid-thirteenth century, after Valdensianism had scattered but also expanded, the French Dominican Stephen of Bourbon (*c.*1200–61) described Valdes's followers in southern France and Lombardy as 'infectious' and dangerous, especially because of their ability to disguise their views. However, he seemed to imply that they imbibed most of their heretical ideas from others, by which he presumably meant the Cathars. As they suffered increasing persecution, and became steadily more alienated from the Catholic Church, the Valdensians rejected its hierarchy and sacraments and its system of prayers and offerings for the souls of the dead. It appears, though, that their doctrines originated from dissent within the Church, on the earlier model of Henry of Le Mans and Peter of Bruys, rather than any outside source. The same could certainly not be said of the Cathars.

There seems now to be no serious doubt that the Cathar groups which developed in southern France and northern Italy in the twelfth and thirteenth centuries derived in large part from dualist movements in Eastern Europe, which appear to have developed in parallel with one another. Like its Western successors, the Bogomil movement seems to have begun, in mid-tenth century Bulgaria, as a group of Christians who lived an austere and simple life but probably did not hold views similar to those of Mani (see chapter 1). By the time that missionaries from Bulgaria were first reported in Western Europe, in the eleventh century, Bogomil ideas had seemingly changed, and their followers in the West, including apparently the heretics of Monforte in 1028 (see chapter 1), were definitely dualist in their views. The earliest known organised Catharism in Western Europe is reported in

Cologne, in 1143, when a Cathar bishop and his companion were tried there for heresy. The poet and mystic Hildegard of Bingen (1098–1179) took great exception to the Cathars in Germany. In 1163, when Eckbert of Schönau, a brother of her friend Elizabeth, was mounting a renewed campaign against what he believed to be highly organised Catharism in and around Cologne, the future saint reported a vision in which Cathars appeared as one of the evils which were unleashed onto the world by the devil, according to the last book of the New Testament, John the Divine's Book of Revelation, or Apocalypse. This occurrence of Catharism in Germany seems to have resulted from both Byzantine Greek and Bulgar missions in the first half of the twelfth century, but divisions between the Cathar churches in those countries were to be reflected all too faithfully in southern France and northern Italy, where the dualistic belief took hold most strongly. A clear and concise account of Cathar beliefs and practices, including their institutional organisation, comes from the pen of Rainier Sacchoni. Sacchoni, a native of Piacenza, abandoned Catharism in 1245, became a Dominican friar, worked as an inquisitor with Peter of Verona, and then succeeded him as inquisitor of Lombardy, when Peter was assassinated in 1252, thus becoming the first martyr of the Inquisition, known to history as 'Peter Martyr'. Sacchoni, like many converts throughout history, seems to have come to hate his former Cathar brethren. His treatise makes a clear distinction between differing groups and doctrinal positions within the Cathar churches. Cathars held Mani's views on the duality between God's good creation and Satan's evil one, as well as the necessity of a spiritual baptism, or *consolamentum*, if a person's soul was to escape the endless cycle of sinful sexual reproduction. Cathars, of whatever congregation and persuasion, were to abstain from meat and dairy products, being the results of coition, though medieval biological theory, based on Aristotle, allowed them to eat fish, which were believed not to reproduce in that way. In addition to their most important service, the *consolamentum*, the Cathars were said to have an equivalent of the Catholic Mass, a communion service which imitated Jesus's actions at the Last Supper but took place (as on that original occasion) in private houses. The Cathars had no churches, but they practised public confession, as had been the custom in the early Church, and had a kind of hierarchy, which was not a priesthood but had one bishop, who was assisted by two elders known as the Elder and Younger Sons (*Filius Major* and *Filius Minor*). There were also Cathar deacons, who helped to lead services, while the faithful were divided into *perfecti* (the *Catharoi* or 'Perfect Ones'), who had received the *consolamentum* and lived the full Cathar faith, and the ordinary faithful, who were under a less rigorous discipline but were required to support the *perfecti*, who acted like travelling pastors. According to Sacchoni, who clearly wished to place his former brethren in the worst possible light, the main problems within the Cathar fold were doctrinal differences over the dualistic faith and, more crucially perhaps in pastoral terms, doubts over the validity of the 'clerical' leaders who carried out the vital sacrament of *consolamentum*. In contrast to the practice of the reformed papal and clerical Church of the thirteenth and subsequent centuries, not only were Cathar orders held to be invalid if the bishop, elder or deacon in question committed sin subsequently to his ordination, but also all the ordinations or other sacraments in which the person in question had taken part were thereby declared invalid. Thus a *consolamentum* might be invalidated, and a soul condemned once more to the cycle of reincarnation in the devil's world.

Despite extensive research, it is impossible to know how many people in the areas that were most influenced by this new Catharism in the late twelfth and early thirteenth centuries became either 'Perfect Ones' or ordinary believers (*credentes*). What is not in doubt, however, is that the papacy, as well as the local Church authorities in southern France and Italy, regarded the Cathars as a much greater danger and, to begin with, the main agents of repression against them were White Monks of the Cistercian order. In 1098, Robert of Molesme founded a monastic community at Cîteaux in France, and within fifty years or so there were well over 300 Cistercian houses throughout Western Europe, the number expanding to more than 740. The early Cistercians aimed to return to the simplicity of the sixth-century monastic rule of St Benedict, but although they strove for complete with-drawal from the world they attracted vast numbers of recruits and also gained considerable influence in the higher councils of the Church. In particular, Bernard of Clairvaux (1090–1153) became a leading spokesman for orthodoxy and reform, alongside Peter the Venerable of the older-established and rival order of Cluny. Other leading agents of the cause were the canons of the Premonstratensian order, which had been founded in 1120, at Prémontré in northern France, by Norbert of Xanten (*c.*1080–1134). Both orders were evangel-ists on behalf of the official, hierarchical Church, with the dual aims of combating heresy within it and uniting Western Christians for the crusade against Islam. The bases for the campaign against heresy in the twelfth and thirteenth centuries were the sharp and precise definitions of what was 'orthodoxy' and what was 'heresy', the reduction to almost nothing of the role in the leadership and liturgy of the Church of lay Christians (from the Holy Roman Emperor down) and the ending of the spread of the Christian faith by any means outside the structures of the institutional Church in general and the monastic cloisters in particular. Thus by the time of the Second Crusade in 1147, 'heresy' had been defined, for the rest of the Middle Ages and into the modern period, by Bernard and the Cistercians, Peter the Venerable and the Cluniacs, the Premonstratensians, and secular canons such as Eckbert of Schönau. These monks and clerics achieved their task by reducing the plethora of beliefs and practices that had evolved in the late Roman and early medieval period to strict and precise *capitula*. These propositions, largely drawn up by themselves became the main criteria for determining orthodoxy throughout the subsequent history of the Inquisition. Thus after around 1160, there were effectively two monoliths, one called 'The Church' and the other 'Heresy'. In practical terms, after Innocent III became pope in 1198, Cistercians were given a leading role in combating the Cathars and Valdensians of southern France and northern Italy. Southern France, known as Languedoc, was an area of fragmented political authority, in which the kings of England and Aragon had direct interests in addition to the king of France, and in which local rulers, in particular the counts of Toulouse, were effectively independent. In this climate of political 'dissidence', religious dissidence prospered too, and by 1172 there appears to have been a Cathar 'bishopric' in Albi, which seems to have led believers in that region to become known as 'Albigensians'. Soon after his accession, Innocent attempted to take the matter in hand. Though his predecessor Alexander III had sent some legatine missions to the region, it was only in 1204 that Innocent appointed Arnald-Amalric, abbot of Cîteaux, to join the existing legate, Peter of Castelnau. The Cistercian monks, whose order was in any case in crisis because of what some of its members perceived to be a falling short of its original ideals, achieved little success, with Cathars and Valdensians continuing to be active, and the local authorities, including diocesan bishops and the count of Toulouse, Raymond VI, largely refusing to co-operate. Peter of Castelnau excommunicated the count for refusing to join a league which he had established in order to secure the peace and suppress heresy. On 8 January 1208, Peter was assassinated, apparently by an overzealous follower of Count Raymond. The pope immediately declared a crusade against the count which was eventually to lead to the subjugation of most of southern France to rule from the king in Paris.

In the meantime, two Spanish clerics visited Languedoc and began a new phase in the Church's struggle against heresy, which was to lead to the establishment of a new, specialised Inquisition. In 1203, Diego bishop of Osma passed through the region on a diplomatic mission from the Castilian king to Denmark. In his retinue was a young canon of Osma cathedral called Domingo de Calaruega, who was to become known in Church history as St Dominic, founder of the order of friars known as Dominicans, Black Friars, or the Order of Preachers. Both men became so concerned at the strength of heretical groups in southern France that they begged Pope Innocent to be allowed to join Catholic missions, either there or in Central Europe. Bishop Diego was sent back to his diocese, but Dominic remained in France, and attempted to improve on the methods of the Cistercians, whom he regarded as too pompous and detached from the people. Like them, he saw the battle against heresy as primarily intellectual, but he felt that monks were too isolated from the world for their arguments to have an effect on the rulers and people of Languedoc. It seemed obvious to him that if Catholics were to bring Cathars and Valdensians back into the fold, they would have not only to defeat the 'Perfect Ones' in theological debate, but also imitate or surpass them in the poverty and simplicity of their lifestyle. Although Dominic's approach was much more intellectual, he thus matched his contemporary Francis of Assisi in his attachment to 'Lady Poverty'. As an accompaniment to military action in Languedoc by largely French forces, under the command of Simon de Montfort, Dominic and his growing band of brothers moved through the region, debating with Cathar leaders and preaching to their supporters. In 1215, the Dominicans received support and accommodation from Bishop Foucher of Toulouse, and five years later the first chapter of the order met in Bologna. In the meantime, the Fourth Lateran Council, which opened in Rome in November 1215, particularly addressed the problem of heresy. Its third canon, or resolution, stated that all those who refused to accept the Catholic faith, as expressed in the Council, should not only be excommunicated but also be handed over to the secular authorities for punishment. Although the nature of the penalty to be exacted was not specified, confiscation of all property was to be automatic, the goods concerned going to the secular ruler, in the case of lay people, and to the Church itself in that of clergy. It was recognised, indeed obsessively in the minds of the growing band of specialised heresy-hunters, that most dissidents were unlikely to reject the Catholic faith publicly when in the presence of the authorities. Innocent's Fourth Lateran Council therefore established procedures for people who were only suspected, but not convicted, of heresy. One was the traditional early medieval practice of 'compurgation', in which 'oath-helpers' were gathered by the accused to testify to his or her innocence. Those suspects who failed to 'purge' themselves in this way within a year of being accused would be automatically excommunicated and treated henceforth as though they had been convicted of heresy. The net was thrown wider than this, however. In view of the longstanding conflicts between the popes and secular rulers, some doubt was expressed by Pope and Council as to the willingness of kings to enforce the Church's discipline against heretics. Rulers were thus to be required to take a Christian oath to enforce Catholic discipline in this matter, but humbler people who had been in any way associated with heretics, for example by giving hospitality to Cathar *perfecti* or Valdensian lay preachers, were also liable to arrest, interrogation and punishment as 'defenders' or 'helpers' of heretics.

As the Church tried to enforce the decrees of the Fourth Lateran Council, and the Dominican friars tramped the 'heretical' lands, preaching and debating, Simon de Montfort's largely northern French armies occupied the county of Toulouse, effectively ended the direct influence of the Aragonese Crown in Languedoc, and in the process carried out violent repression of Cathars, including many burnings. Hostilities temporarily ceased in April 1229, when a treaty was signed in Paris whereby Count Raymond VII of Toulouse, who had succeeded his father seven years earlier, agreed to effective control of his territories by Louis IX of France and that he himself would defend the interests of the Church in every respect, including the repression of heresy. It was in this context that the first formal Inquisition, built on so many theological and institutional precedents, was set up by Pope Gregory IX. In 1229, the very year of the Treaty of Paris, commissions, each consisting of one priest and two or more laymen, were set up in the parishes to identify heretics, but the plan failed because the amateur 'inquisitors' were unwilling to denounce their neighbours to the authorities. Clearly, a more professional and 'objective' remedy was required, and four years later it arrived in France, with Pope Gregory's instruction to the Provincial of the Dominicans in Toulouse to appoint members of his order who were qualified in theology to act as inquisitors in various parts of France, from Narbonne in the south to Bourges in the north. In view of the monolithic power which the Inquisition appeared to exercise in later centuries, it has to be stressed that the early Dominican inquisitors in France quite rightly saw themselves as a beleaguered minority. The violence of their activities could be said to match the equally violent resistance to which they themselves were subjected, frequently from the highest ecclesiastical and secular authorities in the areas in which they worked. One of the first inquisitors, Guilhem Pelhisson, recounts with pride cases which seem to the modern reader to display appalling cruelty. In 1234, for example, when the news of their founder's canonisation as a saint reached Toulouse, the Dominicans, including the city's bishop, Raymond of

Miramont, gathered in their convent to celebrate Mass. Before they could adjourn thereafter to lunch, news reached the brethren that an elderly lady, who was suspected of being a Cathar, was on her deathbed, which soon proved to be the case in an unexpected and horrible way. The bishop went to her at once, and as her relatives were apparently unable to warn her, she seems to have thought that he was a Cathar *perfectus* and unburdened her heart to him. As a result, Bishop Raymond condemned her summarily as an unrepentant heretic, she was immediately taken out of her house, still on her bed, and burned to death, and the Dominican brethren returned rejoicing to their lunch, in celebration of their new patron saint, and of this victory against the Devil's work. Although the activity of the Inquisition in its early decades was not always as arbitrary as in this case, it was only very gradually that set legal procedures were established for the operation of its tribunals. Confusion of jurisdiction between the new Inquisition of the friars and the older episcopal tribunals occurred frequently, and it was never entirely clear in this period whether inquisitors could function without the presence of the local bishop's representatives. Nevertheless, procedures, based on the debating practices of the new universities and on the precedents of canon, or ecclesiastical law, did slowly develop in the second half of the thirteenth century.

When things began to run more regularly, inquisitors, as their name implied, might seek out heresy as well as responding to denunciations. Increasingly accompanied by court officials who included a notary, they would visit a parish or area where heresy was suspected, and have the local clergy call the people together, usually in the main church of the district. A sermon against heresy and in favour of Catholic doctrine would then be preached, and the people would be urged to confess not only their own errors but also those of their friends and relations, within an interval of thirty or forty days. Confessions within this period were intended to lead to minor ecclesiastical penalties and reconciliation to the Church. This apparently joyous moment of restoration to the fellowship of the members of Christ's body, as described by St Paul, was soon to become a way of sorrow to match the austerity and apparent cruelty of earlier penitential rites. The severity of the life of 'volunteers' in the reformed monasteries of the eleventh and twelfth centuries was to be visited upon unsuspecting lay Christians who had made no such choice. For if evidence of erroneous belief and practice had not been given to the inquisitors in due time and form, the forms of inquest and debate, which had been refined in the monastic and cathedral schools, and spread to the mushrooming state bureaucracies, fell with full force on those suspected of heresy. If justice gradually ceased to be as summary as it appears to have been in the first 'crusading' years of the Dominican Inquisition in Languedoc, its long-term effect was as great as ever. The battle against Catharism, and to a lesser extent Valdensianism, in southern France lasted well into the fourteenth century, and produced one of the most skilled episcopal inquisitors of the old school, Bishop Jacques Fournier of Pamiers, whose interrogations succeeded, among other things, in laying bare the social relations of the Pyrenean village of Montaillou. The Inquisition's newly developed expertise spread its effect to other countries and groups, such as the Wycliffites or Lollards, in fourteenth and fifteenth-century England, and the Hussites in fifteenth-century Bohemia, but, in the meantime, the Papal Inquisition had arrived in Spain.

It seemed inevitable, especially given the long-standing dynastic interest of the Aragonese royal house in southern France, especially in Montpellier, that Cathar and Valdensian ideas would spread down the coast into Catalonia. Already, in October 1194, Alfonso I had declared in a council at Lleida that heresy was *lèse-majesté*, a direct and therefore treasonable offence against the Crown. In the early years of the thirteenth century, Alfonso's successor Peter I, who was eventually to suffer a spectacular defeat by the French at Muret in 1213, oversaw increased inquisitorial activity by bishops' courts, but it was his successor James I who followed up Gregory IX's measures of 1232–3, and allowed the establishment of 'professional' tribunals of the Inquisition within his domains. From then on, the battle against heresy in Catalonia and Aragon followed the pattern in much of the rest of Western Europe. The neighbouring, and much larger, Crown of Castile would not become fully involved for several decades more, by which time Jews and newly converted Jews, rather than heretics from within the existing Church, had become the main focus of fear and repression.

3

JEWS AND CONVERSOS
IN SPAIN TO 1478

Conflicts between Jewish Christians and converts from other religions are already recorded in the New Testament Scriptures. The Apostle Paul held that Gentile, that is non-Jewish, Christians should not have to be circumcised if male, or keep the Jewish Law (Torah), for example in dietary matters. As Paul's views came to prevail, it can be seen with hindsight that a split between the new Christian Church and Judaism was inevitable, yet his own view was that the Jews none the less remained God's 'Chosen People', as the Hebrew Scriptures stated (Romans 9–11). During the first and second centuries of the present era, texts which eventually formed the New Testament, such as the four Gospels and the later Epistles, record an increasingly acrimonious and violent conflict between a now largely Gentile Church and Judaism. In this situation, the position of followers of Christ who had formerly been Jews became particularly difficult, and the entire history of Jewish-Christian relations in medieval and modern Spain, including that of the Inquisition, was to be dominated by this problem. From the beginning of the second century, when 'orthodoxy' was being defined against 'heresy' in the Catholic Church, Christian writers began, despite Paul's earlier qualms, to portray Jews and Judaism in an almost uniformly negative manner. Jews were now seen as killers of God Himself, because of their role in the Passion and death of Christ, and they were called, following Jesus's words as recorded in John's Gospel [8:44], children of the Devil. Despite the fact that the Hebrew Scriptures were still regarded by Christians as divinely inspired and revealed, all other Jewish influence was increasingly expunged from Church life. Treatises by distinguished theologians and pastors who were later to be numbered among the 'Fathers of the Church', or Patristic writers, such as Origen (Alexandria, *c.*185–254) and John Chrysostom (Constantinople, *c.*347–407) branded Jews as enemies of the human race, and a whole new genre of anti-Jewish works (in Latin, *Adversus Judaeos*) developed in the early medieval Church. In the West, Augustine of Hippo (see chapter 1) became, for most churchmen, the main authority on how Jews were to be treated. The main 'problem' for the Church was that, as it expanded, largely within the late Roman Empire and its successor states in the West, Judaism refused to die. Despite the destruction of the Temple at Jerusalem by the Romans, in AD 70, and the gradual transition of most of the Empire from paganism to some form of Christianity, Jews continued to reside, and practise a developing and vibrant Judaism under the leadership of non-priestly rabbis and centred on syna-gogues and the home, all round the Mediterranean and further afield. As well as sorting out his own religious identity in relation to Christian 'heresies' in his own time, Augustine felt constrained by the facts of history and by Scripture to face up to the reality of Judaism, in shared Scripture and in relation to the Jews of his own day. Despite the more violent and sometimes paranoid rhetorical excesses of some of his contemporaries as Christian leaders, and it should be remembered that the Bishop of Hippo was himself a master rhetorician, Augustine felt constrained to recognise the ongoing vitality of Judaism and its continuing ability to make converts from the pagan population and even from the ranks of the Christian faithful. Augustine's stance thus reflected a war on two fronts. Against anti-Catholic heretics, some of whom rejected the Old Testament on the grounds that the Christian religion should be entirely spiritual, he affirmed, like Paul, that the Jews had indeed been the Chosen People of God. However, against his Jewish contemporaries he asserted that they were blind and misguided in their rejection of Jesus as Son of God and Saviour of the world. Yet Augustine did see a positive role for the Jews of his own day and of the future. Their continued adherence to the Law (Torah) which represented the covenant made between God and Moses on Mount Sinai, even though this had been superseded by the new covenant sealed by Christ's redeeming sacrifice made for all mankind on the Cross, was none the less divinely ordained. Jews were to be a sign and warning, both to embody the reality of past history and by their present failure and degradation to strengthen Christians in their faith. For this reason, Jews living in Christian society were to receive only reduced human rights, but they were not to be killed, or to be converted en masse to Christianity, until, in God's good time, the world was brought to an end with the second coming of Christ and the Last Judgement.

During Augustine's lifetime, between 370 and around 430, the western provinces of the Roman Empire disintegrated, and numerous successor states were gradually formed. In 376, the Germanic tribe known as the Goths was first admitted to the Empire. By 484, not only had they sacked Rome (410) but the part of the Gothic people which was known as the Visigoths had taken complete control of the Iberian Peninsula, having suppressed other Germanic invaders, the Vandals and the Suevi, as well as the Hispano-Roman population. Between the late fifth century and the Muslim invasion of 711, Hispania, or Spain, was ruled by a succession of Visigothic monarchs from Toledo, which became the ecclesiastical as well as the secular capital of the kingdom. Initially, the Visigothic rulers adopted, and attempted to impose on their subjects, a version of Christianity known as Arianism, after Arius (d.336). Arius was probably a Libyan and is said to have rejected the notion, which became part of the Catholic creeds, that Jesus was fully God as well as man on the grounds that, even before his ministry on earth, he must have been created by His Father. In 587, after much debate among clergy and laity, King Reccared converted to Catholicism, and Spain's considerable Jewish community, which survived from Roman times, came under increasing pressure after, at the Third Council of Toledo (589), sixty-two bishops condemned the Arian 'heresy' and legislated to enforce Catholic orthodoxy. The Visigothic kings were unusual, among the rulers of the 'Barbarian' kingdoms, in retaining within their territories the Roman emperor's right to legislate for their subjects, thus achieving a considerable degree of continuity with the previous system. They also worked closely with the bishops to enforce orthodoxy among their subjects and, during the seventh century, their anti-Jewish decrees, which were promulgated by Church

Councils held in Toledo, grew ever more repressive and extreme. From the conversion of Reccared onwards, the main object of Visigothic legislation in this area seems to have been to bring Spain's Jews into the Christian fold. The Third Council of Toledo (589) decreed that Jews were not to have Christian wives or mistresses, own Christian slaves, or hold public office. King Sisebut (reigned 612–21) passed a probably ineffective law which commanded all Jews to be baptised at once as Christians, while the Sixth Toledo Council (638) stated that the current ruler, Chintila (reigned 636–9), wished no-one to live in his kingdom who was not a Catholic Christian. In his secular law code of 654, King Recceswinth outlawed essential Jewish practices, such as circumcision, dietary laws, marriage rites and the celebration of the Passover. In 694, during the reign of Egica (687–702), all the Jews of the kingdom were legally enslaved, apart from those in the province of Narbonnensis, on the north-eastern frontier with France. Questions have been raised about the motivation for these laws and about their effectiveness. The Visigothic authorities seem not, to put it mildly, to have been very secure in the Catholic faith, and there are grave doubts about the effectiveness of legislation which may betray its irrelevance by its very severity and repetitiveness. None the less, this attempted repression, exercised by a weak and declining state, had two long-lasting effects on Spanish history. Firstly, the Visigothic legislation against the Jews provided unfortunate precedents for the later Middle Ages, and secondly, the story of quite understandable Jewish enthusiasm for a change of government, in the early eighth century, created for the future the long-standing and dangerous legend that the Jews had handed Spain over to the Muslims in 711.

In late April 711, the Muslim commander Tariq, acting on behalf of the Umayyad Caliph of Damascus, Walid I, led a small force across the narrow strait that separates North Africa from Spain. He occupied the rocky promontory which to the Greeks and Romans had been one of the Pillars of Hercules, and which ever after has been known by the name of its Muslim conqueror, Gibraltar, or *Jebel al-Tariq*. It is unclear whether Tariq's original intention was to invade Spain or simply to carry out a raid, but his success was so spectacular that his immediate commander, Musa ibn Nasayr, based in modern Tunis, soon brought over a larger military force to join him. The Visigothic opposition was feeble and divided, and Muslim forces soon captured not only the former Roman colony of Córdoba but also the Visigothic capital in Toledo. Within three years, the whole Iberian Peninsula, apart from its northern and western fringes, was transformed into part of the lands of Islam, which henceforth stretched from modern Iraq to the Spanish Atlantic coast. Initially, Muslims from Arabia, Syria and North Africa ruled Spain through an emirate, but in 959 a separate Caliphate was set up, with its capital in Córdoba, lasting only until 1031, when Islamic rule became fragmented once more. After 711, the small Muslim elite in Spain ruled over a Christian majority and a Jewish minority population, according to principles which had been evolved earlier as the followers of Muhammad (*c.*570–632) moved out of Arabia into the sophisticated Graeco-Roman cities of the eastern Mediterranean and North Africa. The basis for co-existence between Muslims and the other 'Peoples of the Book', the Jews and Christians who share common spiritual origins with them in the patriarch Abraham, and also veneration of the Hebrew Scriptures, had already been established in the East, before the Islamic conquest of Spain began. 'Umar bin al-Khattab, who succeeded the Prophet Muhammad himself as Caliph of the Faithful between 634 and 644, gave his name to a pact with Jews and Christians which was probably in fact made by 'Umar II, who reigned between 717 and 720. This Pact of 'Umar, which was supposedly first made in Damascus, provided the basic framework for relations between Muslims and the Jewish and Christian populations of their domains throughout the medieval period and into modern times. Under its terms, Jews and Christians, as 'protected peoples' or *Dhimmis*, were allowed freedom of worship, and rule in religious and some social matters by their own rabbis or bishops. They were not, however, to build new synagogues or churches, but only to repair existing places of worship, which were not to be higher than neighbouring mosques. Perhaps most significant for the lives of Jews and Christians under Islamic rule, in Spain as elsewhere, was a provision, which certainly did originate with Caliph 'Umar I, that the minority faiths should pay, in addition to other dues, a poll-tax, or *jizya*, which was not demanded of the Muslim faithful. Between the eighth and tenth centuries, a slow process of conversion to Islam seems to have taken place among the non-Muslim population of most of Spain, but without direct persecution or violence, except in isolated cases, such as that of the Córdoban martyrs, including St Eulogius, who were executed in that city, for blasphemy against the Islamic faith, in the mid-ninth century. In the meantime, in the north of the Peninsula, a Christian counter-attack was already under way, which was to be known to history as the 'Spanish Reconquest'.

Because the Muslim invasion never succeeded in controlling the whole of the Iberian Peninsula, the possibility always existed that Christians who had never been conquered might at least attempt to regain the lost territory. In the event, by 1040, when the Caliphate of Córdoba had already broken up into small kingdoms or emirates, known as *taifas*, about a third of the surface of the Peninsula had already returned to Christian rule. The southward advance started on the northern Cantabrian coast, around Cangas de Onís, which fell into Christian hands as early as 722. During the eighth and ninth centuries, this little Christian foothold developed into the kingdom of Asturias. At this time, the beginnings of the later kingdoms of Navarre and Aragon were to be found, in the western and central foothills of the Pyrenees, respectively. In the north-east of the Peninsula, modern Catalonia, the Frankish empire of Charlemagne and his successors annexed territory which became known as the 'Frankish March', a buffer zone between Christian Europe and the Islamic world. In the early ninth century, just when Charlemagne was setting a limit to Muslim power in nascent Catalonia, Spanish Christians further west began a highly significant move southwards, from the damp and green Cantabrian mountains onto the dry Meseta, or central plateau of the Peninsula. This migration, more than all the others, made large-scale Christian expansion southwards a real possibility, and, by the end of the twelfth century, the medieval kingdoms of Castile and León had developed.

The society which evolved in the newly (re-)conquered regions was inevitably dominated by the need for constant military preparedness, as well as an equally militant Catholic Christianity, which was forged by the need for strength and vigilance against the military force of Islam, and the theological power of Judaism. The newly conquered frontier towns received charters (*fueros*, or *furs* in Catalonia), which remained at least theoretically in force into the early modern period. Although they may be described, like the budding states which issued them, as 'feudal' in the most general sense, they were only to a limited extent hierarchical in character. Much of northern Spain in this period was sparsely populated and largely uncultivated, though it was periodically criss-crossed by Muslim and Christian raiding parties. As in the American West of the nineteenth century, settlers tended to arrive before royal bureaucrats and churchmen. In these frontier circumstances, it was impossible in practice to make what was becoming, in most of the rest of Europe at the time, a fairly rigid social distinction between knights, who fought on horseback, and peasants or 'villeins' who cultivated the land and occasionally acted as infantry. The Spanish frontiers thus evolved the novel concept of *caballeros villanos*, or 'villein knights', who spent part of their time trading or working the land, and part of it fighting on horseback. These frontier towns, and their hinterland which increased by stages between the ninth and the twelfth centuries, were not, however, homogeneously Christian, and the 'Reconquest' ideology that was forged at this time and influenced the whole later history of the Spanish Empire had to find a place for both Muslims and Jews.

In some respects, pragmatism was the order of the day. In the twelfth and thirteenth centuries, for example, the use of municipal or privately owned bath-houses in Castilian and Aragonese towns was organised by both gender and religion. In Teruel in Aragon, for instance, Christian, Jewish and

Muslim women appear to have shared the baths on Mondays and Wednesdays without religious distinction, while in numerous towns Christian men bathed separately from male Jews and Muslims. Attempts were made in some cases to grant use of the baths to Muslims and Jews on Fridays and Saturdays, while in Teruel and nearby Albarracín, the public baths were closed on Sundays 'in honour of the Resurrection'. In contrast, as the mid twelfth-century customs, or *usatges*, of Barcelona make clear, severe restrictions, on the model of long-standing Church legislation, were placed on social, and especially sexual, contact between Christians, Muslims and Jews. There were heavy fines for any Jews or Muslims who tried to attract those who had converted to Christianity back to their old religion. As for sexual relations, while a certain latitude was allowed by municipal charters to Christian men, Christian women were liable to be burned if caught in 'fornication' with a Jew or a Muslim. In Soria, they would be subjected first to an inquest, or 'inquisition', and they were commonly liable to flogging and expulsion from the community if they gave birth as a result of such a liaison. These restrictions were reflected in Jewish law, which was severe on both men and women who had sex outside marriage, especially with a Gentile, while Muslim law punished women but not men. These laws and the religious and social prejudices which they represented were to be deeply influential in the history of Spain in subsequent centuries.

From the second half of the eleventh century onwards, the Christian war against Islam in Spain became a part of the general Western European movement known as the Crusades. Campaigns began to receive papal blessing, and both native and foreign troops who took part in wars against Muslims in the Peninsula received spiritual benefits, or 'indulgences', that is a reduction in the time that their souls would spend in Purgatory after death. At the same time, monks from the reformed French orders, and particularly from Cluny, entered Spain and co-operated with Christian rulers in bringing the Spanish Church into line with the latest developments north of the Pyrenees. Most notably, in 1085 Alfonso VI of Castile and León (*c.*1040–1109) succeeded in capturing the former Visigothic capital, Toledo, and this important symbol of the Reconquest became a centre of social and cultural exchange between Christians, Jews and Muslims. During the twelfth century, Muslim political power in the Peninsula was revived by two successive militant dynasties from North Africa, the Almoravids (1090–1146) and the Almohads (1157–1212). After their success at Toledo, the Christian states became increasingly disunited, until, on 16 July 1212, an impressive alliance of Castile-León and Aragon-Catalonia, led by their respective rulers, Alfonso VIII and Peter II, together with some foreigners, achieved a spectacular victory against the Almohad forces at Las Navas de Tolosa, and thus opened the way to the Muslim heartland in Andalusia. Although further divisions, together with the death of Peter of Aragon on another front, at the hands of Simon de Montfort's anti-Cathar crusaders in the battle of Muret in 1213, prevented the Christians from immediately exploiting their success, an inexorable trend had been established. During the thirteenth century, all three Christian frontier states expanded southwards: Portugal into the Algarve, Castile-León into western Andalusia, including the capture of Córdoba, the former Muslim capital, in 1236, and

Seville in 1248, and Aragon-Catalonia into the kingdom of Valencia. The resulting frontier with the newly founded Muslim kingdom of Granada was to remain almost static until Ferdinand and Isabella's victory in 1492. It is conventional, in some circles, to describe the period between 1000 and around 1350 as a 'Golden Age' (succeeding that supposedly experienced by Jews under Muslim Umayyad rule in the ninth and tenth centuries) of co-existence, in Spanish *convivencia,* under Christian rule between Christians, Muslims and Jews, in the sense of tolerance of religious difference and a lack of persecution and violence. The provisions of Spanish legal codes between the eleventh and thirteenth centuries have already demonstrated that such tolerance was severely limited, if it existed at all. But the main figure who is commonly put forward as an example and symbol of medieval Spain as a 'land of three religions' is King Alfonso X, known as 'the Wise' or 'Learned' (*El Sabio*), who ruled Castile-León between 1252 and 1284.

Alfonso X took full advantage of Spain's growing contact with Europe north of the Pyrenees to absorb the increasingly fashionable 'imperial' notions of how monarchs should rule, which were developing particularly in France and Germany. In 1257 he even unsuccessfully put himself forward as a candidate for election as Holy Roman Emperor. In reality, Alfonso's reign in Castile was full of conflict and generally unsuccessful. Even his great seven-part law code, the so-called *Siete Partidas*, was rejected by the Castilian parliament, the Cortes, and not legally promulgated until 1348. Nevertheless, its very coherence and comprehensiveness serve to illustrate the prevailing conceptions of religious difference and dissidence, and how they should be treated. The basic political thought behind the *Partidas* and Alfonso's other legal productions, such as the Royal Charter (*Fuero Real*), was that the king directly represented God to his subjects, and therefore had complete responsibility on His behalf for their religious and social well-being. Significantly, in the sections of the *Partidas* that concerned Muslims and Jews, the drafting closely followed the thought of the noted Dominican canonist, and advocate of the Inquisition, (St) Raymond of Penyafort (*c*.1180–1275). The severe laws on sexual relations across the boundaries of religious communities were strongly reaffirmed, and although litigation within such communities was left to Jewish or Muslim judges as appropriate, Alfonso reserved to Christian courts all legal cases which crossed the religious divide. In terms of faith and practice, the *Partidas* reaffirmed religious freedom for Jews and Muslims who, unlike Christians, were not subject to the Inquisition's jurisdiction, though the code treated Jews as a remnant which had to be 'suffered' by Christian rulers, on Augustinian lines, while Islam was described as 'an insult to God'. Traditional laws restricting the building of synagogues and mosques were repeated, and the ban on Jews and Muslims seeking converts (proselytism) remained in force. More ominously for the future, Jews and Muslims were forbidden to possess books which attacked Christianity, they were to suffer severe penalties if they blasphemed against the Christian religion, even during games of dice, and they were held to be capable of kidnapping Christian children in order to kill them ritually, though no Spanish evidence for this accusation was adduced. Christians were, of course, encouraged to make conversions, though not by force, and measures were enacted with the aim of preventing Jews and Muslims from enticing or coercing new converts back to their former faith. These laws were the slippery slope that was, in later centuries, to lead to direct intervention by the Inquisition in Jewish and Muslim communities.

The 'long' fourteenth century, between 1280 and 1410, has commonly been regarded as period of political, social and economic crisis in Western Europe. In the case of Spain, while the Castilians were attempting to consolidate their huge territorial gains of the period 1212–50, and Aragon-Catalonia was building up a maritime and trading empire in the western Mediterranean, including the Balearic islands, Sicily and Sardinia, there was considerable political and social conflict in both realms. In addition, the Peninsula was affected in the earlier decades of the fourteenth century by natural disasters and epidemics. Iberia seems largely to have escaped the famines which wrought havoc in much of the rest of Western Europe between 1315 and 1317, but the 1330s and 1340s saw bad harvests and epidemics in several years, as well as the effects of the climatic change of the period to generally colder weather. In 1351, the bubonic plague known as the Black Death, which had been sweeping across Europe since 1347, finally reached the Peninsula. In most countries, the plague, which had been spread by black rats, killed at least a third and more probably a half of the population. It used to be thought that in Spain and Portugal only Catalonia, in the north-east, had suffered on this scale, but it is now apparent that the devastation was general throughout the Peninsula. As elsewhere, the massive reduction in population led to frequently violent adjustments in political, social and economic relationships. Minorities, and in particular the Jews, were to suffer especially in these strained circumstances.

In the mid- to late fourteenth century, all the kingdoms of the Iberian Peninsula, though least of all the Muslim kingdom of Granada, were involved in almost constant warfare on three distinct but overlapping levels. Firstly, the 'Crowns', or grouped territories, of Castile and Aragon were engaged in a struggle for domination of the Peninsula, which was fought by both diplomatic and military means. Secondly, from the 1340s onwards, Spain and Portugal were sucked into the conflict between England and France that is known to history as the Hundred Years' War, and thirdly, in the 1350s and 1360s, there was civil war in Castile, as the reigning monarch, Peter or 'Pedro the Cruel', sought unsuccessfully to defend his throne against his bastard half-brother, Henry, Count of Trastámara.

During that war, in May 1355, Henry's forces occupied Toledo and attacked the Jewish quarter known as the Alcaná. Although this might in normal circumstances be construed as a typically violent act of medieval siege warfare, in which the restraints of 'just war' doctrine were held not to apply, in this case it is clear that Jews were the specific and premeditated target. There was a political reason for attacking Jews, in that Henry and the rebels were at the time justifying their efforts to overthrow the legitimate king by accusing him of being excessively favourable to the non-Christian minorities. In the event, Henry, with French help, won the civil war and became king after murdering Pedro during supposed 'negotiations', in a tent at Montiel near Toledo, on 13 March 1369. It seems to be no coincidence that Toledo itself, where the anti-Jewish assault had taken place, fought on against the usurper until June of that year. Although the new Trastámaran regime soon returned to the policies of the former

Burgundian dynasty, and continued, despite protests from the representatives of the larger towns in the Cortes, to employ Jews as administrators and tax-collectors, a dire precedent had been set. With hindsight, it is clear that conditions for Jewish life deteriorated fairly steadily from the moment when Henry of Trastámara adopted the dubious accusation that his opponent excessively favoured Jews as an instrument to achieve political power. It is true that anti-Jewish sentiment had been evident, not least in Castile, during the difficult first decades of the fourteenth century. In 1312, the Church Council of Zamora had incorporated the latest Catholic restrictions on Jews into the law of the kingdom, and Cortes protests against Jewish tax-collectors and money-lenders had multiplied during the reign of Peter's predecessor Alfonso XI (1312–50). In addition, Peter's conspicuous support for the building of a new synagogue in Toledo by the royal chief treasurer, Samuel Halevi, in around 1357, after Henry's attack on the city's Jewry, may have heightened already strong feeling in some quarters, but the case for the king's 'judeophilia' is at best unproven. What is not in any doubt is that anti-Jewish feeling was expressed increasingly strongly during the political and social upheavals in Spain in the last three decades of the fourteenth century, and that in the summer of 1391, Christian-Jewish relations in the Peninsula entered a new and sinister phase.

In that year, the archdeacon of Écija, Ferrán Martínez, was administrator during a vacancy of the wealthy and powerful archdiocese of Seville. He was already notorious for violently anti-Jewish preaching, but in 1391, perhaps because the inter-regnum granted him greater power and freedom, he succeeded in inciting actual physical violence against Seville's

Jews. Between 6 June and mid-August, a wave of violent attacks on Jewish communities in towns and cities swept from Andalusia in the south-west to much of northern and eastern Spain. Jews in Seville, Córdoba, Ciudad Real, Toledo and Logroño in Castile, and Orihuela, Alicante, Valencia, Barcelona and Jaca in Aragon-Catalonia, suffered loss of property, fire, violence and murder. Most of the inhabitants of these communities, or *aljamas*, either fled from the larger towns to smaller centres of population or else converted to Christianity. Those who remained as Jews were subjected, both in Castile and in Aragon, to legal, political and social measures, which put pressure on them to go to the baptismal font. Missionary work was undertaken, in which the Valencian Vincent Ferrer (1350–1419), a Dominican friar who was canonised as a saint as early as 1453, took a leading role, with support in both Castile and Aragon. In 1413–14, a formal theological disputation between Christians and Jews was held in the coastal town of Tortosa, under the auspices of the anti-pope Benedict XIII (d.1423). Yet there is a mystery in that although great anti-Jewish prejudice had been building up in Catholic Europe during the preceding centuries, and earlier evidence in various countries shows that the trickle of converts from Judaism to Christianity had normally been badly treated, the tens of thousands of Iberian converts between 1390 and around 1420 seem to have transferred relatively easily to the Christian majority. According to the models established by the monastic and papal reformers of the eleventh and twelfth centuries, which followed those of the Church Fathers before them, conversion to Christ was not something achieved simply by the act of baptism, but a long, difficult and painful process. Augustine himself even likened God to a 'laughing torturer', a concept which was to be further developed by inquisitors. The converts from Judaism, called *confesos* or *conversos* in Spanish, initially entered numerous sectors of society which had previously been closed to them, including public office, higher education and the trade guilds, as well as the Church itself. This superficially happy situation changed, however, when a revolt occurred in 1449, once again in Toledo. The supposed issue was excessive taxation which had been levied by the government of John II of Castile, through his constable Alvaro de Luna. The house of a converso tax-collector, Alonso de Cota, was attacked and then the assault was extended to the large converso community of the city. The leader of the rebellion, Pero Sarmiento, and his legal adviser, Marcos de García Mora, nicknamed Marquillos, issued a so-called 'Sentence-Statute' whereby all conversos were henceforth to be excluded from public office, because of their Jewish origin. Although the Crown quickly restored order, and Pope Nicholas V (reigned 1447–55) condemned the rebels and their statute of 'purity of blood' (*limpieza de sangre*), the notion that the Jewish Christians of Spain were still tainted by Judaism and not to be trusted was not to leave Spanish society for many generations. In the meantime, a campaign arose for an Inquisition to settle once and for all the question of whether the conversos were really Christians or still Jews. A ferocious debate on the subject ensued, involving numerous churchmen, academics and politicians.

As John II (reigned 1406–54) was replaced as king of Castile by his son Henry IV, who succeeded him between 1454 and 1474, political turmoil continued in Castile. The main conflict was between factions of the upper nobility, who sought to control the wealth and patronage which were at the disposal of the Crown. In addition, though, attacks were mounted on conversos, for example in Ciudad Real in 1467 and in Córdoba in 1473 and 1474, with the aim not only of looting their property but also of excluding them from public life on the grounds that they were still Jews in reality. During this period of turmoil, in 1469 King Henry's half-sister Isabella married Ferdinand, the heir to the Aragonese throne, and prepared to ascend the throne of Castile in highly dubious circumstances. The new 'Spanish Inquisition' was about to become a reality.

4

THE NEW SPANISH INQUISITION

Ever since the rebel 'purity of blood' statute had been introduced in Toledo in 1449, the religious character of the
conversos had been a political issue. In the civil conflict of
Henry IV's reign in Castile, anti-converso agitation often
focused on their exclusion from public office, on the overt
grounds that their Jewish origins made them untrustworthy,
but in reality as an instrument of faction conflict. In 1465, the
manifesto drawn up by a group of rebellious nobles, against
the king and in favour of his young half-brother Alfonso,
went so far as to demand the introduction of an Inquisition
to Castile. By this time, the conversos, rather than the
kingdom's remaining Jews, were regarded as the main enemy.
In accordance with the demands of the ecclesiastical propagandists of the previous two decades, the nobles asked that, if
specialised inquisitorial tribunals were not to be set up,
diocesan bishops should themselves take responsibility for
rooting out 'Judaising' heresy. Sometimes, the threatened
conversos responded violently. On Sunday 19 July 1467, for
example, a group of armed conversos invaded Toledo
cathedral, during the high mass, accusing those present of not

being true Christians, and a major riot followed two days later. After this uprising had been defeated, similar disturbances further south in Ciudad Real led, in June 1468, to confirmation by the king of all 'Old Christian', or non-converso, office-holders in posts which had been seized from Jewish Christians. On 14 July 1468, Henry granted Ciudad Real a statute excluding conversos from municipal office, thus apparently accepting the argument which had been put forward by the Toledo rebels in 1449. Although the converso bishop Juan Arias Dávila of Segovia condemned between eight and seventeen Jews to death in 1471, for supposedly committing the ritual murder of a Christian child, the main target of political and social hostility in the last years of Henry IV's reign in Castile continued to be the conversos. In the Andalusian city of Córdoba, this period saw a violent conflict between two branches of the Fernández de Córdoba family, one led by the count of Cabra and the other by Don Alonso de Aguilar. The perception grew that Don Alonso, who as the city's chief magistrate (*alcalde mayor*) had succeeded in expelling the leaders of the Cabra faction, excessively favoured conversos, in public and economic life, and even in the Mosque-Cathedral itself. Opposition to his rule focused particularly on a religious confraternity, known as the Brotherhood of Charity (*Cofradía de la Caridad*), membership of which was restricted to 'Old Christians' who claimed to have no Jewish blood in them. In March 1473, the brothers were marching in procession, accompanying a statue of the Virgin Mary, through the predominantly converso streets at the southern end of the Calle de la Feria, which was the north–south axis of the city and a major centre of economic activity. As the procession was passing the intersection which is still known as La Cruz del Rastro, a young girl dropped some liquid from the balcony of a converso house onto the statue. It was probably water, and an accident, but the brothers immediately decided that it was urine, and therefore a deliberate insult by a Judaiser to the Virgin. A leading member of the confraternity, the blacksmith Alonso Rodríguez, rallied both brothers and bystanders to wreak vengeance on the conversos of the neighbourhood. Initially, some Córdobans, led by a squire (*escudero*), Pedro de Torreblanca, whose family held public office in the town, attempted to stop the violence, but Pedro was wounded, and rioting and looting continued until Don Alonso himself arrived. Rodríguez was inveigled out of sanctuary in the nearby Franciscan church of San Pedro el Real (known as San Francisco), but the chief magistrate stabbed him with a lance during 'negotiations'. The blacksmith, near to death, was taken home by his supporters, and it was soon announced that he had died but had then been miraculously resurrected. With the help of this spiritual reinforcement, the rioters went to work with renewed vigour. Attempts by Don Alonso himself and by a city councillor (*veinticuatro*), Pedro de Aguayo, to protect the conversos failed, and the chief magistrate was driven out of the eastern half of the town, the Ajerquía, and took refuge in the castle (Alcázar). Some conversos were sheltered in the neighbouring 'Old Castle' (*Castillo Viejo*), but others were killed or wounded, many houses were burned and a large amount of property was looted. When the main violence started, on 16 March, workers from the surrounding countryside were involved as well, and some hundreds of conversos fled to smaller towns in the province, or as far as Seville and Gibraltar. Some even emigrated to Italy or

Flanders. In the meantime, Don Alonso de Aguilar allowed a statute to be passed in Córdoba which banned conversos from public office, but some conversos either remained in the city or else returned when the violence had died down, as there was a further, lesser outbreak in December 1474.

There is no doubt that the political context of Iberia in the 1470s played a major part in the establishment of inquisitorial tribunals in Castile. At the time when Isabella was proclaimed queen, at Segovia on 13 December, faction conflicts were continuing in many parts of the kingdom, including Andalusia, where the first tribunals of the new Inquisition were to be established. These local struggles inevitably became entangled with the civil war which began in 1475, as the Castilian succession was disputed between Isabella and Henry's daughter Joanna (Juana), who had both been recognised at different times by the Castilian Cortes as heir to the throne. The Andalusian magnates and towns stayed on the margin of the conflict, which began when Joanna's new, and much older, husband, Alfonso V of Portugal, invaded Castile in order to assert her claim. By the end of 1476, however, Isabella had succeeded in gaining the support of most of the leading nobles in Andalusia, and conceived the idea of visiting the region when hostilities ended. Despite the misgivings of counsellors, who felt that she should not undertake such a delicate mission without the presence of her husband Ferdinand, Isabella left Madrid on 20 April 1477. She headed south-westwards into Extremadura, visited the Jeronymite monastery of Guadalupe for the burial of former King Henry, and arrived in Seville on 24 July. Large numbers of its citizens, who feared punishment for their misdoings of the previous decades, fled in advance of her coming. but it soon became clear that the queen was interested in religious as well as political dissidence. Modern scholarship suggests that Isabella's claim to the succession was at the very least no stronger than that of Joanna, who almost certainly was indeed the legitimate daughter of Henry IV, and not the illegitimate daughter of the royal favourite Beltrán de la Cueva, after whom her opponents nicknamed her 'La Beltraneja'. Isabella had no such doubts, of course, at least in public, but she was encouraged to link opposition to her claim to the throne with Judaising among by conversos in Andalusia, by the preaching and advice of the Dominican prior of San Pablo in Seville, Alonso de Hojeda. During her stay in that city, in which Ferdinand had subsequently joined her, both rulers seem to have decided that the long-advocated method of an Inquisition should be introduced to Castile, in order to secure both their own rule and religious orthodoxy.

Between 8 July and 1 August 1478, a national council of the Spanish Church was held in Seville, at which an extensive programme for its reformation was agreed. The sessions took place amidst growing fears of conspiracy and treachery by Judaising conversos. At this time, the archbishop of Seville, Cardinal Pedro González de Mendoza, published a pastoral letter, which was aimed at giving 'New Christians', or conversos, greater knowledge of the Christian faith. He himself joined with his deputy, the bishop of the neighbouring diocese of Cádiz, with the Dominican friars and, after 2 August 1478, with the royal governor, or *asistente* of Seville, Diego de Merlo, in acting against supposed Judaisers. As Cardinal Mendoza's pastoral campaign was put into effect, 1478 saw further lurid accusations of violent conspiracy against Seville's conversos. In the meantime, though, the king and queen were pursuing another avenue, in Rome, and, on

1 November 1478, Pope Sixtus IV (reigned 1471–84) issued a bull which authorised the appointment of two or three priests, who should be over forty years of age, to act as inquisitors in Seville, with the possibility of more appointments in other parts of Castile. Thus the 'professional' Inquisition finally arrived in a part of Europe which had never seen it, in this form, before. Perhaps surprisingly, Sixtus's bull was not implemented for nearly two years. On 27 September 1480, the Crown, which in novel form had been granted power of nomination by the pope, appointed two Dominican friars, Juan de San Martín and Miguel de Morillo, to act as inquisitors in the archdiocese of Seville and diocese of Cádiz, with Dr Juan Ruiz de Medina as their assessor. Martín had previously been Prior of the Dominican house of San Pablo in Burgos, and also vicar of the 'Observant' or reformed congregations of the order in Castile. Morillo had only in the previous year been elected Dominican Provincial of Aragon, apparently with the support of the new king, Ferdinand, and Dr de Medina, a secular cleric, was a member of the Castilian Royal (Privy) Council. On 1 January 1481, the new Seville Inquisition issued a letter to all the nobles of Andalusia, asking them to co-operate in its work. The authorities in the main towns, which were under direct royal jurisdiction, could evidently be relied on, but there were doubts about areas in which jurisdiction had been granted to nobles by the Crown. In the case of Seville itself, the city's chief royal representative, the *asistente* Diego de Merlo, immediately took an active part in the tribunal's work. By the end of 1480, many conversos had fled, and lurid and provably false accusations of converso plots to destabilise the city and its government were circulating. To begin with,

the inquisitors set themselves up in Hojeda's Dominican convent of San Pablo, but in 1481 they moved across the river Guadalquivir to the large castle of Triana, of which Merlo was the governor on behalf of the Crown. On 11 February 1482, Pope Sixtus IV issued a further bull, whereby seven more Dominican inquisitors were appointed, including the Prior of Santa Cruz in Segovia, the soon to be notorious Fray Tomás de Torquemada, and the new tribunals began to spread across Andalusia and Castile. The first of these was established in Córdoba, where violence between political factions had only recently been quelled. On 4 September 1482, the chapter of the Mosque-Cathedral granted permission to Pedro Martínez del Barrio, Bachelor Alvar García de Capillas, and Bachelor Antón Ruiz de Morales, who had been appointed inquisitors in Córdoba diocese by pope and rulers, to absent themselves from choir services while carrying out their duties. By the time the Cordoban tribunal began to function, the actions of the Andalusian inquisitors had stirred up major controversy, both in Spain itself and in Rome.

Contemporary chroniclers estimated that, between 1481 and 1488, 700 Judaisers were handed over to the secular authorities and burned, either in person or in effigy, while approximately 5,000 were 'reconciled' to the Church, that is restored to full membership, in return for various penances. Whatever the accuracy or otherwise of these figures, it appears that the first Spanish *auto de fe*, an 'act of faith' or procession and public humiliation of penitent or impenitent 'heretics', took place in Seville on 6 February 1481, soon after the inquisitors began their operations in Triana castle, extending their tentacles to other towns in the region, such as Jerez de la Frontera and Puerto de Santa María. The introduction of the Inquisition to Castile remained highly controversial, however, and the debate within Spain over the real existence or otherwise of Judaising among the conversos, soon reached the pope in Rome, in the form of complaints about perceived abuses by the new inquisitors. On 29 January 1482, Pope Sixtus wrote a letter to Isabella and Ferdinand, in which he alluded to various examples of misconduct by San Martín and Morillo in Seville, and complained that the new foundation was not a 'true' Inquisition, because it was specifically targeting supposed Judaisers, and was not a general inquest into heresy. Nevertheless, the work of the Seville Inquisition and its equivalent in Córdoba was not interrupted. Indeed, the new tribunals which had been authorised by Sixtus IV in February 1482 were gradually established. In the summer of 1483, the introduction of an inquisition was announced in the Andalusian city of Jaén, and another in Ciudad Real, in New Castile, where violence between conversos and 'Old Christians' had occurred in earlier years. Two years later, this tribunal moved north to Toledo, where it quickly had an impact on the lives of the city's numerous converso population. By the time that Jews who refused to convert to Christianity were expelled in the summer of 1492, there were also, within the Crown of Castile, inquisitorial tribunals further north, in Ávila, Medina del Campo, Segovia, Valladolid and Sigüenza. Despite a certain amount of political controversy, and some alleged converso plots in both Seville and Toledo, these organisations had gone about their work with relatively little overt opposition. The situation when the new, royally sponsored Inquisition, now under the leadership of Torquemada, was introduced to Ferdinand's Crown of Aragon, was to be very different.

The fundamental problem was, of course, that an Inquisition already existed in the Crown of Aragon, having been established in the thirteenth century. As early as 1481, Ferdinand took steps to gain greater control over the existing Papal Inquisition in Aragon, Catalonia and Valencia. Inquisitors who had been appointed by the king, rather than the pope as formerly, began work in Saragossa, Barcelona and Valencia, and a powerful converso lobby soon gained support against them from Pope Sixtus IV, in the form of a bull dated 18 April 1482. This document accepted the truth of converso stories about inquisitorial abuses, and instructed bishops' officials to take part in the work of the inquisitors, so as to act as a check on them. Strong diplomatic pressure, from Ferdinand himself and from his ambassadors in Rome, quite soon produced a change of heart on the part of the pope, however, and on 17 October 1483 Sixtus appointed Torquemada as Inquisitor General of Aragon, Catalonia and Valencia. This was a daring and highly controversial innovation because, up to this point, there had been no legal or institutional link between the 'Crowns' of Castile and Aragon. One of the many violent constitutional storms in the history of the Aragonese and Catalan kingdoms was about to break out. As ruler of these eastern territories, Ferdinand inherited a complex legal and constitutional structure of charters or *fueros/furs* which vested more authority and power in the various parliaments, or *Cortes/Corts*, of the Crown of Aragon than in the king or his ministers. When parliament was not sitting, a Grand Committee, or *Diputación/Diputació*, carried on the government in his name. The initial resurrection of the medieval Inquisition in these realms had threatened the conversos, but had not raised constitutional questions. The appointment of Castilian inquisitors to territories in which the *fueros* required all officials to be natives was quite another matter. Thus the violent opposition to what was rightly perceived as Ferdinand's 'new' Inquisition, which broke out all over the Crown of Aragon in 1484–5, had two distinct origins. Naturally, conversos, many of whom were prominent in royal and municipal government, fought to preserve their status as sincere Christians against accusations of Judaising which might very well lead to punishment and death, if Torquemada's new and vigorous tribunals, which had already demonstrated all too clearly what they could do in Castile, were to begin work on the other side of the border. However it is clear from the events of these years in, for example, Saragossa, Teruel, Barcelona and Valencia, that there was also a constitutionalist and anti-Castilian basis for opposition to the new Inquisition, which was capable of uniting a much wider constituency. Although all resistance eventually proved futile, in the face of the king's absolute determination to match his wife's policy in this matter, it had seemed initially that the new inquisitors might be defeated by a combination of legal complications, political intrigue at the highest level, both in Spain and in Rome, and in some cases violence and even murder. The legal difficulties were not only concerned with the problematic appointment of Castilian officials in the Crown of Aragon, but also with the embarrassing existence of inquisitors who had been appointed under the old papal system to serve in Barcelona and Valencia, and who would have to be removed. On 14 April 1484, Torquemada held a meeting, or *junta*, in the Aragonese town of Tarazona, where the Cortes of the kingdom was assembled at the time, and announced the appointment of inquisitors to investigate and punish 'heretical depravity' in Saragossa, Huesca, Teruel, Lleida, Barcelona and Valencia. At the beginning of May, Gaspar Juglar and Pedro Arbués de Epila were named as inquisitors in the kingdom of Aragon and despatched to the capital, Saragossa, where they immediately met the opposition of a united front of conversos and 'Old Christian' constitutionalists. Their colleague, the young Basque Dominican Juan de Solivera, at first could not even enter the legally autonomous Aragonese town of Teruel, when he arrived there on 23 May 1484. Having been warned by their returning representative (*procurador*) at the Cortes of Tarazona, the local council had already gone into secret session with its lawyers to work out the constitutional basis for resisting the Inquisition. Thus fortified, the councillors refused Solivera admittance to the town, and the young friar, who, being under forty, was too young to exercise the office of inquisitor in the terms of royal legislation and Torquemada's instructions, as the notoriously obstinate and legalistic Teruel councillors were quick to point out, was forced to retire ignominiously to the nearby town of Cella, where his colleague, Martín Navarro, was vicar. The population of Teruel at this time was a mixture of Christians, Jews and Muslims and, although there was a prominent converso group among the citizen body, it is clear that the unifying factor in the town's stout resistance was the defence of its constitutional liberties. When Ferdinand, through his official representative, the Capitán Juan Garcés de Marcilla, crushed all opposition, so that Solivera and Navarro could finally enter the town on 25 March 1485, he was following, in his contempt for the town's traditional freedoms, the precedent of his uncle Alfonso V. In 1427, during a dispute, Alfonso had ordered the chief municipal legal officer, the Judge (*Juez*) to be hanged, and his body to be thrown out of a window of the town hall onto the main square. Between 1484 and 1487, Teruel was to see its converso community purged, like those of so many other towns in the Crowns of Castile and Aragon.

Resistance to Ferdinand and Torquemada's new Inquisition was no more effective elsewhere in the king's domains. In Barcelona, an inquisitor, Joan Comes, had been appointed by the pope at the city's request in 1461. Because of this, the Catalan capital did not even send representatives to Tarazona in 1484 to discuss the introduction of the new Inquisition, but this refusal did nothing to stave off the reality of Ferdinand and Isabella's Spain. Resistance in Barcelona was legal rather than violent, but it was no more successful than other methods used elsewhere. The city's councillors refused to accept Torquemada's nomination of two new inquisitors and revocation of Comes' commission, but Ferdinand fully backed his Inquisitor General and prepared to ride roughshod over the *fors*. During 1485, numerous conversos, including some of the wealthiest citizens, fled the city, and it was in the following year that a legal device was found whereby Comes could be removed and a new tribunal set up. In February 1486, Pope Innocent VIII formally removed all inquisitors, old and new, in the Crown of Aragon. In the case of Barcelona, this enabled Torquemada to replace Comes with a new Castilian appointee, the Dominican Alonso de Espina. His harvest of burnings and reconciliations was limited, though, as most of the likely converso victims had fled. In Valencia, to the south, two inquisitors, Juan Cristóbal de Gualves and Juan Orts, had been appointed by the pope under the old dispensation as recently as 1481. Although one of the replacements appointed in 1484 by Torquemada was a Valencian named Martín Iñigo, the other was Juan de Epila, an Aragonese, with the result that the Cortes of Valencia raised immediate protests that their *fueros* had been violated by the appointment of a non-native. Once again, the opposition campaign was unsuccessful, and the city and kingdom of Valencia duly succumbed to a king who argued that, if there really were little or no heresy in his realms, then his subjects had nothing to fear from the new tribunals. What proved to be the violent, self-inflicted defeat of resistance to Ferdinand and Torquemada's Inquisition took place in the capital of Aragon, Saragossa.

The Inquisitor Pedro Arbués de Epila knew that his life was in danger from a deadly combination of the hatred of influential conversos and equally powerful defenders of Aragonese constitutional rights. As he prayed before the high altar of Saragossa cathedral on the night of 15–16 September 1485, he wore a coat of mail under his robes and steel under his clerical cap. It was not enough. According to contemporary accounts, eight men, hired by some of his converso enemies, crept up to him, verified his identity, and one of them stabbed him. After receiving further wounds, he lingered for about a day more, before becoming the first 'martyr' of the new Spanish Inquisition, on the pattern of his thirteenth-century predecessor, Peter Martyr. The effect of this murder, together with the all-too-ready identification of its instigators, ruined the hopes of conversos not just in Saragossa itself but throughout Spain, and severely damaged efforts to defend traditional constitutional rights in Aragon and the Catalan lands, including soon the Balearic islands.

Now that the new tribunals were established in most of Isabella and Ferdinand's possessions, how did they proceed with their task of 'extirpating' heresy?

Under the influence of later fictional accounts, in various languages, inquisitors have often been seen as wild-eyed fanatics, devoted to sadistic cruelty, yet it is extraordinarily difficult to gain any real impression of the character of Torquemada's first inquisitors. Whatever evil they did seems all too banal, and the details known about them are the typically sketchy biographical fragments of the period. Even Torquemada himself is known, like most of those who were interrogated by his tribunals, from external actions rather than his inner character and motivation. Brother Solivera was accused by the councillors of Teruel of having a foul temper, but they were hardly impartial, and the worthy friar may to some extent be excused a little impatience and frustration, from his own point of view, given his opponents' ponderous and determined obstructionism. Later, in 1508 (see chapter 5), the then inquisitor of Córdoba, Diego Rodríguez Lucero, was to be effectively convicted of grossly illegal conduct and truly sadistic violence towards numerous inhabitants of that town, but such 'human' insights are all to rare in the period. If the surviving evidence is to be believed, most Spanish inquisitors in the late fifteenth and early sixteenth centuries were largely faceless bureaucrats rather than spectacular tyrants. They were all clerics, many of them were Dominican friars, and their academic training was more commonly legal than theological. The recorded operations of Isabella and Ferdinand's tribunals largely confirm this impression.

The new Spanish Inquisition followed its medieval predecessor in being an uneasy combination of a law court and a confessional. The official aim of the Holy Office had always been to reconcile wandering souls to the Church. In that sense it was a part of the sacrament of penance or reconciliation, whereby a sinful believer might confess his or her sins to God, in the presence of a priest, and then receive advice aimed at amendment of life, a penance, and absolution, which meant that previous sins were wiped out, and a new start made. In many respects, the thirteenth-century Inquisition and its successors adopted similar procedures. In late fifteenth-century Spain, as elsewhere in earlier centuries, the normal first requirement of an inquisitor, when he and his entourage arrived in a place where heresy was suspected, was that the people of the district should confess their sins, and particularly in matters of belief. There was, however, an important difference, in that individuals in these circumstances were required to confess not only their own 'sins' but also those of others, their relatives, friends and neighbours. It was here that the confessional became a law court, or rather a police court, since the Inquisition sought to discover networks of those involved in the anti-social activity of religious dissidence. In terms of legal basis and practice, the new 1478 foundation in Spain not only followed the provisions of existing canon law, which continued to be amended by both papal and royal legislation, but also adopted two fourteenth-century procedural manuals for its day-to-day operations. The first was composed by a French Dominican, Bernard Gui (1261/2–1331), and is generally known as the *Manual of the Inquisitor*, while the second, which continued to be highly influential well into the early modern period, was written by a Catalan from the same religious order, Nicolau Eymerich (1320–99). Both were directed primarily against the heresies of their own day, including Catharism, Valdensianism and the dissident groups in the Franciscan order who were known as 'Spirituals'. Ominously for later developments in Spain, they also identified the dangers of Jews and Judaism in general, and of lapsed Jewish converts to Christianity in particular. Apart from the greatly enhanced role of the king and queen in their appointment, the main innovation in the operation of the new Spanish inquisitors and their officials was the introduction of defence counsel for the accused. It remained to be seen how effective this safeguard would be for the thousands who were hauled before the tribunals of the Holy Office, in the reigns of Ferdinand and Isabella and their successors.

5

THE SPANISH INQUISITION, THE CONVERSOS AND THE JEWS

The debate about the work of the Spanish Inquisition during the reigns of Ferdinand and Isabella continues to be lively, as academic conferences and publications proliferate both within and outside Spain itself. The not inconsiderable archives of the Inquisition, which have survived destruction and dispersal in later centuries, have been studied methodically ever since Henry Charles Lea published at the beginning of the twentieth century his pioneering, and still valuable, four-volume history of the Spanish tribunals. Yet some fundamental facts are still not known, and the void tends to be filled by polemical assertions, often based on the religious and secular ideological preconceptions of the twentieth century. Much of this debate and polemic has been about numbers. How many Jews were there in late fifteenth-century Spain? How many conversos were there? What proportion did these two groups form of the total population? How many Jews left the country in 1492 and how many converted at once or returned later as Christians? All these questions are closely linked with the work of the Inquisition, but they are not generally susceptible to statistically based answers. For one thing, there was no

Protestant cruelties inflicted on Catholics, from a work by Joannis Baptista Cavallerius, published in Rome in 1584.

systematic census of the Spanish population until the reign of Charles V. As in other European countries, Spanish tax-lists, which might have provided a partial substitute, were organised by household rather than individuals, so that an arbitrary demographic 'multiplier' has to be used to estimate population. Worse, Jews and Muslims in the Spanish kingdoms, who are so crucial to any soundly based assessment of the work of the Inquisition, were taxed globally, as communities, so that only the crudest calculations can be made from the relative size of the tax burden placed by the Crown on each. The working guess is that there were about 6 million people in Spain in the late fifteenth and early sixteenth centuries, three quarters of them living in Isabella's Crown of Castile, and the rest in Ferdinand's Crown of Aragon. The proportions of this estimated population who were Muslims, Jews or Jewish Christians (conversos) are, as will be seen, a matter of intense controversy, but it is probably safe to say that altogether they did not amount to more than about 10 per cent of it, in other words 600,000, but this too is a risky assumption. To those contemporaries who debated the early work of the Inquisition, however, statistics, at least in the modern sense, were not the main consideration.

Controversy arose as soon as the inquisitors started work in Seville. The royal chronicler Fernando del Pulgar, who was himself a converso, protested in early 1481 to his patron, the archbishop of Seville Cardinal Pedro González de Mendoza, against the indiscriminate accusation and arrest of conversos, on the grounds that, while a minority of them might deserve punishment as Judaising heretics, it would be cruel and unjust to persecute the rest. Pulgar did not, however, make the same assumption as the modern scholars Benzion Netanyahu and Norman Roth, that this majority of the conversos were sincere faithful Christians. While that might be true in many cases, the chronicler also pointed out that many female conversos, especially in Andalusia where the new Inquisition began its work, were not conscious Judaisers but simply ignorant of Christianity, because they were largely enclosed in their houses and no-one had taught it to them. The inquisitors, and their royal and ecclesiastical backers, were not deterred by such protests and continued their deadly work. As has been noted (see chapter 4), in Seville, contemporary writers estimated that between 1481 and 1488 approximately 700 Judaisers were tried by the Inquisition, many in their absence. Those who had not fled were made to process in an *auto de fe* and then burned as 'relapsed' heretics by the municipal authorities. In the Inquisition's own jargon, this process was described as 'relaxation to the secular arm'. Absentees who had been convicted in this category were burned in effigy, though this did not, of course, absolve them of being burned in person if they were ever caught. In addition to Pulgar's doubts, in January 1482, Pope Sixtus IV himself responded to converso complaints by instructing Isabella and Ferdinand to suspend the Seville inquisitors while supposed abuses were investigated. The objections of Sixtus, and of his successor Pope Innocent VIII (reigned 1484–92), did not prevent continuing activity by the new tribunals, both in Castile and in Aragon. In Córdoba, for instance, the now fragmentary records for this period show that the inquisitors soon began, in 1482, to organise trials in the city's main royal castle, the Alcázar, which were followed by *autos de fe*, at least once each year between then and 1486. After the 1483 *auto*, at the nearby Benedictine convent of the Holy Martyrs (*Santos Mártires*), the supposed mistress of the Cathedral treasurer, Pedro Fernández de Alcaudete, was burned outside. Further north, in Ciudad Real and then Toledo, the bulk of the existing converso community was systematically humiliated, while a similar process was undertaken by the new tribunals in Aragon, Catalonia and Valencia. There is no doubt that conversos were the primary targets of the early inquisitors. It is estimated, on the basis of the extensive surviving records, that over 90 per cent of those tried by the new tribunal in Valencia, between the beginning of its work in 1484 and 1530, were conversos, and the available evidence suggests a similar picture in the areas covered by other Castilian and Aragonese tribunals.

Given the perceived political and social emergency in which Ferdinand and Isabella set up their new Inquisition, it was perhaps inevitable that the procedures under which it worked should largely have imitated those set out for its medieval predecessors by papal legislation and Nicolau Eymerich's fourteenth-century manual. As in earlier cases where a specialised Inquisition was at work, both in Spain and abroad, the first sign of an investigation into supposed heresy was normally the publication of an 'edict of grace', which gave the population of the place where it was proclaimed an interval of thirty or forty days in which to confess their sins. As in the case of the medieval tribunals, a 'full' confession involved the denunciation of others, and might enable the inquisitors to penetrate what they perceived to be 'networks' among heretics. In Córdoba, for instance, Diego Rodríguez Lucero, who worked as inquisitor in the city from 1499 until 1508, when he was dismissed for abuse of his office after an exceptional investigation conducted on royal authority, believed (almost certainly falsely) that secret synagogues were operating, with a network of congregants that reached into the highest echelons of local society. After the initial onslaught against the conversos had abated, Spanish inquisitors tended to travel less frequently through their districts in search of heretics, but rather they increasingly remained in their headquarters to await the reports and initial investigations of their outlying commissioners (*comisarios*), who were frequently local clergy. Thus, after around 1500, the issue of the edict of grace by itinerant inquisitors was replaced by the annual reading of an 'edict of faith', which omitted the interval during which it was possible, at least in principle, to confess one's sins and be reconciled to the

Church without suffering physical or financial penalty. Whichever form of edict had been proclaimed, and whatever the eventual outcome, the financial consequences of arrest on suspicion, or after confession, of heresy were immediate. The tribunals of the Spanish Inquisition, despite their political dependence on the monarchy, were institutionally self-financing, and the movable and immovable property of the accused was confiscated at once by the local tribunal's 'receiver', who then administered it with a responsibility for the relatives and retainers who might otherwise face immediate ruin. Almost at once, in Castile, Aragon and Catalonia, the accusation became widespread that the inquisitors were more interested in the wealth of rich conversos than in a search for Judaising heresy – a *sacadinero*, money-extraction or 'rip-off', some called it. It was exceedingly rare for such property to find its way back to its original owners, and if it did, the Inquisition made sure to claim full administrative expenses. In most cases, the property was auctioned to provide funds for the local tribunal concerned. Meanwhile, the arrested suspects began their ordeal, which was generally long and painful and which ended almost universally in public humiliation in an *auto de fe*, and sometimes in death by burning.

When the Inquisition had begun its work, in southern France and northern Italy in the thirteenth century, its juridical methods had been part of a lengthy campaign by the Church and monarchies to replace the vagaries of trial by ordeal of sword, fire or water with court procedures that formed the basis of those used ever since. Thus dependence on the direct intervention of God to determine guilt or innocence, through the result of combat, branding with a hot

The arrest of Catholics by Protestants, in the context of the late sixteenth-century Wars of Religion, from Cavallerius.

iron, or ducking in water, was replaced by the giving of evidence in court. This had been unnecessary under the old system, in which the just Judge already knew everything and delivered his verdict in the result of the ordeal, but now, cases were tried by human court officials, who represented earthly hierarchies, whether of Church, monarchy, secular lord or municipality. In some cases, juries consisting of fellow citizens of the accused replaced the old custom whereby someone might defend themselves against charges by producing neighbours as 'oath-helpers', to support them in swearing their innocence. In this way, the prestige of the burgeoning ecclesiastical and secular bureaucracies of Western Europe was increased, but there were two practical difficulties, which had not been fully resolved by the time Ferdinand and Isabella's

A French representation of a Spanish auto de fe.

Inquisition began its work. One of these was the nature and the assessment of evidence and the other was the new practice of sentencing those convicted of secular or ecclesiastical crimes to periods of imprisonment which might be lengthy. The first specialised tribunals, in the thirteenth century, confronted a situation in which imprisonment was not a normal judicial punishment, except when wealthy prisoners of war were kept, usually in castle dungeons, in the hope of being ransomed. There was thus very little prison accommodation available, and sentences of 'perpetual imprisonment' soon became subject to remission. Those sentenced, for example, between 1318 and 1325 by the famous episcopal inquisitor Jacques Fournier (later Pope Benedict XII, reigned 1334–42), in the diocese of Pamiers on the French side of the

Pyrenees, seem rarely to have spent more than a year or two in gaol. Frequently, as in the case of the southern French town of Carcassonne in the thirteenth and fourteenth centuries, castles and fortifications were used as prisons by the Inquisition, and this practice was soon followed by the first two tribunals in Andalusia after 1480. In Seville, as has been noted (see chapter 4), the inquisitors were quickly invited by the royal *asistente* Diego de Merlo to occupy the castle of Triana, which stood forbiddingly at the southern edge of the bridge of boats across the river Guadalquivir, while their colleagues in Córdoba shared the main royal castle in the town, the Alcázar, with the Crown's representative, the *corregidor*. In Barcelona, part of the royal palace was used by the new Inquisition, and it was not until the mid-sixteenth century, notably in Toledo in or around 1560, that purpose-built prison accommodation was constructed. Throughout its existence, the Spanish Inquisition thus faced a shortage of cells which materially affected both its interrogation of prisoners and its sentencing policies.

The question of the validity or otherwise of the voluminous evidence which was collected by the Spanish Inquisition during the 356 years of its existence is as vital to modern interpreters of the tribunal's work as it was to both accusers and accused at the time. It is true that the Inquisition carried out judicial procedures which may be compared directly with those of secular law-courts, as well as the ordinary ecclesiastical tribunals, generally under the authority of bishops, which attempted to administer family law concerned with morals, and in some countries such as England, inheritance law as well. In this sense, it is thus entirely fair to compare Inquisition procedures with those of other courts of the period, and, inevitably and properly, comparisons may be made with later legal practice. But despite its political origins, and its subjection to a considerable degree of royal control, the Spanish Inquisition after 1478 was, like its predecessors on both sides of the Pyrenees, part of the Church's administration of the sacrament of penance, or reconciliation. It has already been noted that, under the terms of the edict of grace or of faith, the inquisitor required those accused of heretical beliefs and practices to make a full confession of all they knew on the subject, concerning others as well as themselves. This was a spiritual as well as a legal matter, so that to withhold information, whether deliberately or accidentally, was to deceive not only the inquisitor but God himself. All lying, whether by commission or omission, was a mortal sin, which affected the eternal destiny of the offender. Heresy, though, and especially leadership of heretical groups, was regarded by the Church and by secular authorities as so serious and dangerous a sin and crime that the normal provision that a penitent who innocently forgot a sin might still be fully absolved did not in practice apply. It is thus not surprising that, as soon as they began work, in Andalusia and then elsewhere, Isabella and Ferdinand's tribunals were accused of abusing their powers and convicting people falsely. Another reason why the procedures of the new tribunals were regarded by many at the time as suspect, as they have been since, is their very 'inquisitorial' nature. Despite the large quantity of excellent scholarship which is now available on the subject, it is still widely believed that the 'Inquisition' was an entirely Spanish, and entirely ecclesiastical phenomenon. Also, despite the entirely valid and complete demolition of the contention by the distinguished Jewish historians, Yitzhak Baer and Benzion Netanyahu, it is necessary to stress once again that there is no worthwhile evidence to support the suggestion made by those otherwise highly distinguished Spanish scholars, Claudio Sánchez Albornoz and Américo Castro, that the origins of the Spanish Inquisition lay in the legal procedures of the Jews themselves. In reality, 'inquisition', or enquiry after truth, became general in the common law of medieval Europe, which developed out of Roman law in and after the twelfth century. It was thus far from being unique to the Church and in medieval England, for example, the standard procedure of legal enquiry on behalf of the Crown into the possessions of deceased persons was known as an 'inquisition post mortem'. The legal process of 'inquisition', whether applied in religious or secular circumstances, differed substantially from modern English and American methods of investigation and trial. As in twentieth-century practice in countries in which Roman law is still influential, in continental Europe and elsewhere, the two main objects of the legal authority in medieval and early modern heresy cases were to establish the truth, and then to apply a pre-existing code of law in order to determine the appropriate penalty for the guilty. One consequence of this set of legal prescriptions and presuppositions was that the evidence was compiled before the 'trial' took place, or rather, that the investigation of the case was itself an integral part of the trial. All this needs to be understood, if the often-vilified procedures of the Spanish and other Inquisitions of late medieval and early modern Europe are to be properly assessed.

Confessions made after the proclamation of the edict of grace or faith led to the accumulation of large quantities of evidence, against those who gave it and against others. Some people effectively surrendered themselves to the Inquisition, while others were arrested by its constable (*alguacil*) and his officers, on the instruction of the relevant tribunal's prosecutor (*procurador fiscal*). This would happen once the prosecutor had convinced the inquisitors that there was a *prima facie* case to be answered. It was at this point that the confiscation of the property of the accused took place, while he or she was incarcerated in whatever prison accommodation was available, flooding being a regular hazard in the basement cells of the Triana castle in Seville, which have recently been partially excavated. Ever since the 1480s, one of the worst abuses of the Spanish Inquisition has been seen to be the secrecy with which it operated. In theory at least, a prisoner accused of heresy was separated, after arrest, from the rest of humanity. He or she was confined in a secret cell, without verbal communication with gaolers, other prisoners, or the outside world, including relatives. Interrogation also took place in secret, within the Inquisition prison, with one or more inquisitors asking the questions and a notary of the tribunal, who was also sworn to secrecy, recording the proceedings. Relatively few of these trial records survive today from the period up to 1530, but those documents which are still extant provide a clear indication of how trials were generally conducted. The prosecutor was required to assemble witnesses against the accused, and draw up a set of charges against them. At no stage was there a confrontation between the witnesses and the accused. Instead, the prosecution witnesses were each required to respond to an identical set questionnaire, based on the charges and often including forty or fifty questions, regardless of their relevance to the particular role of the witness in the case. An important novelty in the procedure of the post-1478 Spanish tribunals was the introduction of a defence lawyer, who at this stage received from the Inquisition fiscal the list of charges and the prosecution evidence. There were, however, two grave limitations on the possibility of an effective defence. Firstly, the defendant had no choice of counsel, but was forced to take the lawyer appointed by the inquisitors. It was evident that the career prospects of practitioners were unlikely to be enhanced by mounting an effective defence of such clients, and few examples are known of the display of moral courage in this type of case. The second major handicap for the defence was that, when the prosecutor handed over details of his case, he withheld all circumstances which might identify the witnesses concerned, including dates and places as well as their names. This was supposedly done in order to prevent later reprisals against those who assisted the Inquisition's work, and their friends and relations. Under this grave disadvantage, the accused and his or her counsel assembled their case and summoned their own witnesses, who also had to answer a set questionnaire. In theory, the inquisitors were bound to discount the testimony of all those who were declared by the defendant to be his or her 'mortal enemies', but this rarely, if ever, proved to be an effective safeguard, as the names of accusers had to be guessed, and one witness not so designated was enough to condemn. In addition, although evidence had to be given in set form during trials (leading to a repetitiveness which is the bane of those scholars who work on trial records!), the inquisitors, who in this respect regarded their court as a confessional, were remarkably undiscriminating in the admission of testimony. In any case, once the prosecution and defence witnesses had given their evidence, and the prisoner had been interrogated, the inquisitors reached their verdict, which was then put to a group of assessors (*calificadores*), who were generally local parish clergy, monks, friars or academics. These advisers might also vet cases before they were brought to trial, and sometimes took up their entitlement to attend interrogation sessions. Once the verdict and sentence had been agreed, the prisoner was presented for public penance in an *auto de fe* ('act of faith').

In the early days, and up to the middle of the sixteenth century, these were austere and brutal acts of humiliation and punishment. For example, in Toledo in the 1480s, hundreds of mainly converso citizens, including some of the wealthiest members of the community, processed barefoot, in white robes and carrying large candles, from the original headquarters of the local Inquisition, in the Dominican convent of San Pedro Mártir (named after the first inquisitor to be killed by heretics, in Italy, see chapter 2), to the main square of the city, the Plaza de Zocodover. Unlike the Nazarenes (*nazarenos*), whose voluntary penance in modern Spanish Holy Week processions is disguised by flowing robes and pointed hoods which cover their faces except for the eyes, the identities of the convicted prisoners of the Inquisition were displayed for all to see. The visible rites of penance and, it was hoped by the authorities, penitence had developed in the Church over many centuries. The Spanish Inquisition developed a new refinement, by dressing its convicted prisoners in tall mitres, as though in parody of episcopal authority, and in yellow robes, known as *sambenitos*, which showed a visual representation of their offences, and which were afterwards hung in the offenders' parish churches, as a sign of infamy for them and their families. The sentences at the Inquisition's disposal included 'mild' traditional penances, which might equally apply to those who had confessed mortal sins to their parish priests, such as compulsory attendance for a period at mass, with ritual humiliation, or compulsory pilgrimages. More serious offenders, in the eyes of the inquisitors, might be 'reconciled' to the Church, but still had to serve, in principle if not in practice, a sentence of 'perpetual imprisonment'. In any case, such people lost all their property, and their families suffered the stigma of being the relatives of convicted heretics. Those who were convicted as 'relapsed heretics', who had previously been reconciled to the Church for heresy and who were, in the delicate phrase of the inquisitors, derived from Proverbs (26:11) and the second epistle of Peter (2:22), 'like a dog returning to its vomit', were paraded in an *auto* wearing a *sambenito* which was 'decorated' with flames. After the ceremony, they were taken away, under the authority of the local magistrates, known in ecclesiastical jargon as the 'secular arm'. After a ritualistic appeal had been made by the inquisitors that they should be mercifully treated, they were put to death by burning, alive if they were unrepentant, and having been first garrotted if they had expressed repentance and Catholic devotion at the stake. Any modern attempt to suggest that the impact of the Inquisition was not as severe as has often been supposed must nevertheless confront the reality of these powers, which were repeatedly used in Spain and abroad during several centuries. What, though, was the religious identity of those convicted by inquisitorial tribunals in the reigns of Isabella and Ferdinand?

The inquisitors of the new Spanish tribunals inherited well-established notions of the nature of Judaism. Following New Testament sources, they regarded the religion of their Jewish neighbours as dead and legalistic, and, worse than that, as something inspired by the devil. It is striking, though not surprising, that the charge-sheets which were drawn up by inquisitorial prosecutors against supposed Spanish Judaisers consist almost entirely of accusations of ritual observance of the Jewish Torah (Law), as well as supposed disrespect of the Christian faith. Even allowing for the formulaic nature of Inquisition interrogations, whether of the accused or of witnesses, there is remarkably little theological discussion, in contrast to the preoccupation with such issues which is evident in controversies elsewhere in Europe at the time, involving, for example, those designated 'Lollards' in England, or 'Hussites' in Bohemia. The inquisitors clearly had a problem, and would occasionally admit it in their private manuals, in identifying the internal beliefs, whether religious in the 'official' sense or not, of their fellow citizens. The temptation to judge by externals was rarely resisted, and many must have been sent by Spanish inquisitors to their deaths, or at least to imprisonment, and financial and social ruin, for buying meat from a kosher butcher, who slew his animals according to Jewish precepts, or for changing their tablecloths on a Friday, as though in preparation for the Jewish Sabbath. Such was the staple fare of thousands of Inquisition trials in the Spain of the 'Catholic Monarchs', but were the tens of thousands of conversos in fifteenth-century Spain really 'Jews' or 'Christians'? In the twentieth century, many scholars, both Jewish and non-Jewish, no longer profess the belief systems which are associated with the terms 'Judaism' and 'Christianity'. None the less, it is very rare to find a student of the affairs of Ferdinand and Isabella's Inquisition who does not largely accept traditional rabbinical or priestly definitions of what constitutes, and constituted, a 'Jew' or a 'Christian'. It is, of course, entirely reasonable to assume as a starting point that Spanish inquisitors, who had been brought up in a society where Jews, Christians and Muslims had co-existed for many centuries, might be expected to have a fairly clear notion of what constituted 'Judaism', even if they had never themselves entered a synagogue, or seen an animal ritually slaughtered, or sat with a Jewish family, who perhaps were relatives, in a hut under the stars during the festival of Succoth. Yet systems of belief, and it was noted earlier that Christianity, on the model of the Jewish Torah, was largely defined, by the creeds and by medieval schoolmen, as a set of propositions to be assented to or rejected, were then as now far more rigid than the actual beliefs and practices of individual people, even if everyone needs some structure in which to live. Recent debate on the religious identity of the Spanish conversos has largely consisted of an artillery bombardment of generalisations and abstractions, with little or no attempt to define the terms used. Thus the conversos were either 'Jews', in which case the Inquisition was justified in its own terms but acting immorally in persecuting those who were in their hearts, if not legally, adherents to another faith, or else 'Christians', in which case they were cruelly persecuted for holding beliefs which they did not in fact hold. The rigid and stereotyped proceedings of Inquisition trials do not easily yield up personal stories, especially in the years of the main onslaught on Judaising conversos, between 1480 and around 1520. There is, however, enough evidence in these and in other sources, such as the pre-trial witnesses' depositions recorded in the registers of the Inquisition of Soria and Burgo de Osma between 1486 and 1502, to indicate that as many basic theological and philosophical options were open to Spaniards in that period as have been available since, and that they were as likely to be exploited then as they have been in the late twentieth century. The Inquisition of the 1480s and 1490s was acting, in the same way as so many modern scholars appear to think when working on the subject, on a monolithic model, which made little or no allowance for confusion or contradiction. The results were to be the expulsion from Spain of Jews who refused to be baptised as Christians, and three more centuries of persecution of those who appeared to deviate, or did indeed deviate, from an official model of Christian belief and practice. However political the purpose of the Spanish Inquisition may have been, its religious self-perception was never abandoned.

6

TRIUMPH AND REINVENTION
OF THE INQUISITION

The initial onslaught of the inquisitors against the conversos, between 1480 and 1492, took place in kingdoms at war. During nearly all of that period, Ferdinand and Isabella mobilised the human and material resources of the Crowns of Castile and Aragon to defeat and conquer the last Muslim-ruled state in the Iberian peninsula, the Nasrid kingdom of Granada. Both Jewish and Muslim communities in their territories escaped attack, whether political or religious, though massive and disproportionate contributions to the war effort were demanded of them. Only later were Spain's remaining Muslims to be pressurised into conversion and hence become targets of the Inquisition. The Christian threat to the Jews was, however, to become visible during the last two years of the Granada war. It began as an apparently routine Inquisition case. In June 1490, some drunks at an inn in Astorga, in north-western Spain, claimed to have found a eucharistic host, the consecrated bread of the Mass, in the luggage of a converso wool-comber called Benito García. The vicar-general or chief representative of the bishop of Astorga, Dr Villalba, was informed, and the suspect was

DE

ORIGINE ET

PROGRESSV OFFICII

SANCTAE INQVISITIONIS,
ciúfque dignitate & vtilitate,

DE ROMANI PONTIFICIS POTESTATE
& delegata Inquifitorum: Edicto Fidei, & ordine iudiciario
Sancti Officij, quæftiones decem.

LIBRI TRES.

*Autore Ludouico à Paramo Boroxenfi Archidiacono & Canonico
Legionenfi, Regniá, Sicilia Inquifitore.*

MATRITI,
Ex Typographia Regia.

cIɔ.Iɔ. xcɪɪx.

The title page of Luis de Páramo's On the origin and progress of the Office
of the Holy Inquisition *(Madrid, 1598).*

immediately arrested and tortured. Owing to a shortage of reliable evidence, there is much dispute over the extensiveness of this practice in the early years of the Inquisition, and it is not clear whether García was tortured by secular or ecclesiastical authorities, but it soon became clear that his case was a matter for the inquisitors. The fullest surviving account of the subsequent trial is in the papers concerning another of the accused, a Jewish shoemaker called Yuçe Franco. The case of the stolen host was initially taken up by the inquisitorial tribunal in Valladolid, but it was soon transferred to Avila, the home town of the inquisitor-general, Tomás de Torquemada. By this time, however, a much more serious accusation was being made, that a group of conversos and Jews, including Yuçe and Benito, had kidnapped and ritually murdered a small boy from the town of La Guardia, near Toledo. Thus was born the story of the 'Holy Child' of La Guardia, which has resonated through the centuries in Spain, and which is still commemorated locally, despite the disapproval of the Roman Catholic authorities. Through the lawyer, Martín Vázquez, who had been appointed by the inquisitors to defend him, Yuçe stated that the charges which had been laid against him by the Inquisition fiscal, Don Alonso, that he was guilty of conspiracy, of crucifying the young boy in mockery of the sufferings of Jesus, and the employment of magical practices (*hechicería*), were too vague and lacked specific dates and other particulars. As has been noted, this was a standard feature of prosecution material when it was handed over to the defence, and therefore an unlikely way out for the defendant, but Yuçe was on much stronger ground when he asserted that, as a Jew, he was not under the jurisdiction of the Inquisition and therefore should not be involved in the case. Here, Yuçe and his lawyer touched on an issue which had vexed the Inquisition ever since its beginnings as a specialised body in thirteenth-century France. In 1320, Bishop Fournier of Pamiers had interrogated a German Jew called Baruch, who had been forcibly baptised by participants in the so-called Shepherds' Crusade in southern France, but he had done so on the basis that the defendant was a baptised Christian and not a Jew, in which case he recognised that he would have had no jurisdiction in the case. The La Guardia case was to blur this distinction in a dangerous manner, as far as Spain's Jews were concerned. In addition to trying Jews as defendants, when previously they had only been summoned as witnesses against conversos, the Avila tribunal, doubtless with the blessing of Torquemada, was about to break many of the rules of practice which had been established by the inquisitor-general's 'Instructions' of 1484.

The 1490 investigations had evidently produced insufficient co-ordinated evidence to convict this group of about ten Jews and conversos of stealing a eucharistic host, and kidnapping and crucifying a Christian boy. When new interrogations took place early in the following year, the story was further elaborated, to include the stealing of the boy's heart for use in a Jewish blood sacrifice, yet the accused obstinately refused to agree among themselves. Frustrated, the inquisitors not only resorted to torture, but also brought the prisoners together in an attempt to make them co-ordinate their story. The Jewish and converso gang was meant to have kidnapped the boy in the midst of a crowd in Toledo, on the Feast of the Assumption, before carrying him off to a cave near La Guardia. In November 1491, after further torture and confrontation of witnesses, the Avila inquisitors obtained the agreement of a local committee of assessors (*calificadores*) that the accused were guilty as charged, and an *auto de fe* was held on 16 November, after which Yuçe and his companions were burned alive. Although some have doubted it, there is a clear and evident connection between the trial and conviction of the supposed murderers of the 'Holy Child of La Guardia', who only later acquired the name Christopher (Cristóbal), the 'Christ-bearer', and the subsequent expulsion of the Jews from the Crowns of Castile and Aragon. On the day after the burnings in Avila, a local notary, Antón González, wrote to the town council of La Guardia, reporting on the behaviour of the condemned men at the *auto de fe*, and effectively inviting the councillors to set up a pilgrimage site where the remains of the 'Holy Child' were found. This did not happen until 1569, but in 1491, soon after the trial itself, the Avila Inquisition ordered that the proceedings should be translated into Catalan, and published in Barcelona. Evidently, the normally secretive proceedings of the Inquisition of Torquemada were to take on some of the trappings of a 'show trial', with the aim of demonstrating that Spain's conversos not only retained close links with their former co-religionaries, the Jews, but also conspired with them to carry out violent and wicked actions against 'Old' Christians, who were not of Jewish origin.

Already, before the trial of the supposed murderers of the 'Holy Child of La Guardia', attempts had been made to expel Jews from parts of Spain. Although the text does not survive, it is evident from other sources that on 1 January 1483 the inquisitors of Seville and Córdoba ordered all Jews in the dioceses of Seville, Cádiz, Córdoba and Jaén, effectively all the part of Andalusia then held by the Christians, to leave within three months, with restrictions on the goods which they could take with them. It has been suggested that the measure was at least in part a security device, aimed at protecting the frontier with Muslim Granada in time of war, but there is in any case no doubt that the initiative came from the Inquisition. Three years later, a similar order was made for the diocese of Albarracín, in Ferdinand's kingdom of Aragon, where the town of Teruel had recently seen sometimes violent confrontation with the new tribunal, and where there was no frontier with Muslim territory. Both the Andalusian and the Aragonese orders were of limited effect. The town council of Jerez de la Frontera protested at the measure. Jews were certainly paying taxes once more in Córdoba in 1485, others received royal licences in the late 1480s to return to Andalusia and resolve their financial affairs, while in Aragon the town of Teruel saw a number of Jews baptised in 1492, when the national expulsion edict was issued. In each case of the issue of a local expulsion order, the explicit intention of the inquisitors was to prevent in the future the personal and religious links between Jews and conversos which they believed to have been revealed by the work of their tribunals throughout Castile and Aragon. Today, bitter controversy surrounds the value, if any, of the evidence which the Inquisition accumulated, in the 1480s and later, of supposed Jewish beliefs and practices among the conversos. For some scholars, notably Benzion Netanyahu and Norman Roth, the conditions under which such evidence was obtained by the inquisitors render the results useless for any other purpose than that of revealing the anti-Jewish prejudices of the inter-rogators. For many others, inspired by Yitzhak Baer, Cecil Roth and Haim Beinart, the testimony accumulated by

Ferdinand and Isabella's inquisitors reveals a deep religious and social identity between Jews and conversos. According to this view, in their own terms, the inquisitors were thus right to regard most conversos as Judaisers. Yet the surviving sources for Inquisition trials in this period display a much more varied and nuanced picture than much of the current debate about the religion of the conversos in the fifteenth century, which seems mainly to thrive on blanket generalisations and attacks on the credentials of opposing scholars. In any case, the inquisitors had no doubts, and used their trial records, and particularly the case of the 'Holy Child of La Guardia', to put pressure on the monarchs to order a general expulsion of unconverted Jews from their territories.

Two versions of the eventual edict, one for Castile in the names of Ferdinand and Isabella, and the other for Aragon in Ferdinand's name alone, were both dated in Granada on 31 March 1492. They ordered, in the differing forms of their respective chanceries, that all Jews who refused to be baptised as Christians within an interval of four months would be forced to leave their sovereigns' territories. They would have to dispose of their houses, and other immovable property, and would only be allowed to take with them into exile goods which were permitted to be exported. Gold and silver coin and bullion, and potential military supplies, such as horses, might not be taken out. In the event, Castilian and Aragonese Jews were given even less than four months to make their fateful decision, because of a delay of nearly a month in the issue of the edicts to local authorities. This seems to have been due to unsuccessful efforts by Jewish leaders in Castile, particularly Abraham Seneor and Isaac Abravanel, to persuade the king and queen to change their minds. Apart from their use

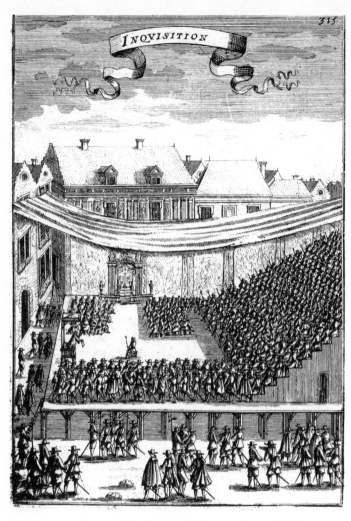

A late seventeenth-century French portrayal of a Spanish auto de fe, *from* Mollat's Description of the Universe.

of different bureaucratic formulae, the Castilian and Aragonese versions of the expulsion edict justified the same basic measures in slightly different ways. The Castilian document referred directly, for example, to the earlier inquisitorial expulsion order for Andalusia, while Ferdinand's Aragonese chancery produced a more stereotyped anti-Jewish diatribe, which stressed the harmful effects of their usury as well as their unfortunate effect on the Christian orthodoxy of the conversos. Both versions explicitly offered the Jews a choice between baptism and removal, but despite, or perhaps in part because of, the mushrooming studies of the subject in recent years, virtually everything connected with the 1492 expulsion is still deeply controversial. To begin with, it is not clear whose initiative was mainly behind the edict of 31 March. The powerful influence of the Inquisition has been indicated already, but the lively controversy, which has gone on ever since their reign itself, concerning the relative power and influence of Isabella and her husband Ferdinand also surfaces in the case of the Jews and their expulsion. Some contemporary sources suggest that the apparent religious fervour behind the edict came from the queen, or at least that Ferdinand sheltered behind it when facing critics of the policy, but there is also a school of thought, going back to sixteenth-century writers on the period including the great Aragonese historian Jerónimo Zurita, which ascribes the predominant influence in the dual monarchy to Ferdinand. The continuing inconclusiveness of this debate is paralleled by controversy over the purpose of the expulsion edicts. Given the explicit terms of the documents concerned, as well as some of their consequences, it seems obvious and understandable that they have become known as 'expulsion orders', which paralleled those made by Edward I of England in 1290, the French Crown at various dates in the fourteenth century, and a large number of European princes and city governments in the decades which preceded 1492. In the summer of that year, the largest Jewish community in Europe followed the example of so many others, in England, France, Germany and Italy, and attempted to dispose of its fixed property at derisory prices. They then set off on a trek, across land or sea, to Portugal or the still-independent kingdom of Navarre, within the Iberian peninsula, or southwards into the Muslim kingdoms of North Africa, or eastwards to Italy or the Ottoman Empire. Both Christian and Jewish sources of the period record, with varying degrees of sympathy, the sufferings of the exiles, which paralleled those of refugee groups in Europe up to the present day. They were forced to take with them only what they could carry, and were abused by Christian neighbours, customs officials and ships' captains. Those who reached Muslim lands in North Africa were frequently set upon and killed, others faced hostility and obstruction in Christian territory, including Portugal and Italy, while those who placed themselves under the rule of the Ottomans appear to have fared better. Thus was created the Sephardic Diaspora (from the Hebrew word 'Sefarad' which is traditionally held to refer to Spain), which has been highly influential in Jewish life ever since. Yet despite the certainty with which some scholars continue to express themselves on the subject, it is simply not possible to establish how many Jews left Ferdinand and Isabella's territories in 1492.

Generally speaking, although nothing has diminished understanding and concern for the sufferings of those who became exiled from their country as a result of the edict of

31 March, estimates of their numbers have been revised downwards in recent years. The impossibility of establishing accurate population figures, for Spain or any other country, in this period has already been noted. Given these limitations, a figure between 70,000 and 100,000, rather than earlier estimates of 150,000–300,000, is probably not wildly inaccurate, so that revisionism has not succeeded in denying that a major human disaster took place. Nevertheless, there is evidence that the offer of the alternative of conversion to Christianity was a genuine one, and that it was taken up by considerable numbers. Evidence from various places indicates that some converted within the time allowed by the Castilian and Aragonese edicts, thus saving their established lives and their property. That their actions were in accord with royal intentions is more than suggested by a document which was issued by Ferdinand on 15 May 1492, ordering Torquemada to ensure that his inquisitors did not deter Jews from converting by threatening them with evidence of their previous links with supposedly Judaising conversos. The major economic and social upheaval took place in the summer months, however, when thousands of Jews departed and a large amount of real estate changed hands. On 10 November 1492, Ferdinand issued a further decree from Barcelona, which explicitly encouraged those who had emigrated to return, on condition that they could prove that they had been baptised as Christians. The document was said to be a response to a petition from Jews who had converted after crossing the border into Portugal, and the king ordered efforts to be made to smooth their return as Christians. They were to be allowed to re-enter Castile through the border towns of Badajoz, Ciudad Rodrigo and Zamora, and might

even do so in order to be baptised in those towns. Once officially Christian, they were to be allowed to return to their home towns and villages, and reclaim their property from those who had bought it, no doubt at much reduced prices, earlier in the year. In what appeared to be a disconcerting provision for those concerned with the stability of the property market, the temporary owners were to be compensated with no more than the cost of any improvements which they may have made to their purchases. Given the 'inclusive' nature of this provision, it is surely not reasonable to assume, as Netanyahu appears to do, that the 1492 expulsion was an ideologically racist measure in terms similar to those employed much later in the Third German Reich. In practice, it is clear from surviving documentation that numerous Jews took advantage of the royal offer and returned to Castile and Aragon as Christians in the latter months of 1492 and during the next few years. It is equally clear, however, that the Inquisition did not show the restraint in such cases which had been advocated by Ferdinand, and many of the returnees soon found themselves subject to its ministrations. The policy battle between Ferdinand and the inquisitors, which continued after Isabella's death in 1504 and seems to have been dominated by questions of finance, led to a confusing and contradictory situation for the Spanish public. While conversos were being investigated and arrested by the Inquisition for supposed Judaising, the Crown was selling documents of 'rehabilitation' (*habilitaciones*) to individuals who sought to have their dealings with the Holy Office expunged from the record. Such ambiguities were to become ever more prevalent in Spanish society as the sixteenth century progressed.

At least chronologically, and no doubt in many other ways too, the edict on Jews of 31 March 1492 was closely connected with Ferdinand and Isabella's conquest of the city of Granada, which officially took place on 2 January of that year. During the preceding war, and particularly in the partial agreements which were made between the Christian and Muslim authorities in the years from 1484 to 1492, political considerations had priority over religious and cultural matters. The heads of agreement (*capítulos*) of the conquest of 1492 corresponded to this pattern. Like its predecessors in the thirteenth century, when the Castilians had conquered western Andalusia and Valencia had been added to the Crown of Aragon, this agreement guaranteed freedom of worship to the population of the former Muslim kingdom. The elderly Jeronymite friar, Fray Hernando de Talavera (bishop 1492–1508), who had been Queen Isabella's confessor and was appointed as the first archbishop of Granada after the conquest, has been fairly regarded as model diocesan bishop, and a practitioner of the Catholic reform which, after the Council of Trent (1545–63), became known as the 'Counter-Reformation'. He seems to have endeavoured to observe both the spirit and the letter of the 1492 *capítulos*, and laboured to convert the Islamic population of the former Nasrid kingdom by example rather than coercion. He attempted to ensure that his clergy learnt Arabic and worked, as did his successors in the post, including Archbishops de Ávalos (bishop 1528–42) and Guerrero (bishop 1546–76), to build up a native Granadan clergy. To use in another way the imagery which was so beloved of earlier persecutors of heresy, the little foxes, which entered and made havoc of the vineyard of Archbishop Talavera and his reforming successors (Song of Songs 2:15), were a renewal of Christian-Muslim conflict and the Inquisition. Although the Holy Office was excluded from the kingdom of Granada until the 1560s, by agreement with both the Catholic Monarchs and Charles V (1526), violent conflict between Christians and Muslims, which appears to have been encouraged by the then archbishop of Toledo, Cardinal Francisco Jiménez de Cisneros (1436–1517), erupted in 1499–1500, and led to inquisitorial action thereafter. The tribunals of Córdoba and Jaén both became involved in the former Muslim kingdom, and Talavera's accommodating policies were largely abandoned. As a final insult, the last major act of the inquisitor of Córdoba, Diego Rodríguez Lucero, before he was investigated and dismissed in 1508, was to accuse the saintly Talavera himself of operating a secret Jewish synagogue in his household. The elderly archbishop died shortly afterwards, and it was only some decades later that a tribunal of the Inquisition was set up in Granada. Forced conversion of the kingdom's Muslims had provided a potential clientele after the uprisings of 1499–1500 in the Alpujarras mountains near Granada, and a similar order applied to Muslims in the rest of the Crown of Castile in 1502 had provided work for existing tribunals. The kingdom of Valencia, which had been conquered by the Aragonese and Catalans in the thirteenth century, still retained a large Muslim population, especially in the countryside. The treaties whereby the conquest was ratified were still in force at the beginning of the reign of Charles V, who felt constrained to swear to keep them at his accession in 1518. Under these terms, freedom of worship was granted to Muslims. Valencian territory was dotted with mosques and the voice of the muezzin continued to be heard in places until as late as 1570. As in the case of Granada, though, pressure for mission and conversion, from the Church in general and the Inquisition in particular, became harder to resist after 1500, both in the kingdom of Valencia and among the smaller Muslim population of Aragon. Traditionally, the rights of the Muslims had been protected by the general Aragonese determination to defend constitutional usage and rights at all costs, and by the desire of the Christian nobility to preserve a docile and dependent labour force on their estates. Castilian influence in the Crown of Aragon had grown greatly, however, under Ferdinand's rule, and the example of the neighbouring kingdom in ordering the forced conversion of its Muslim minority, outside the kingdom of Granada, in 1502, had resulted in added pressure for change. In Valencia, the turmoil of the first years of Charles V's reign produced the revolt of the Germanías ('Brotherhoods') in 1521–2, during which the Christian middle and lower classes protested against royal authority and the power of the nobility, and in addition, numerous Muslims were forcibly baptised. Although this rebellion, like that of the Comuneros in Castile in the same period, was soon defeated, Islam in Valencia was never to be so secure again. After 70–80,000 Muslims in the region had been forcibly converted, thus becoming Moriscos, Charles asked Pope Clement VII (reigned 1523–34) to release him from his 1518 oath to allow the free practice of Islam in Valencia, but the request was refused. Instead, a special commission was set up to investigate the juridical status, in terms of Church (canon) law, of the baptisms which had taken place during the Germanía rebellion. This was chaired by the then inquisitor-general, Alfonso Manrique, and perhaps inevitably, given the nature of European inquisitorial practice going back to the thirteenth century, the validity of the sacrament was upheld in these cases. On 20 October 1525, Charles ordered all Muslims in the kingdom of Valencia either to convert or to leave the territory by 8 December of that year. Although the issue of forced conversion remained controversial for the rest of the century, and the Inquisition was excluded from operations against the Moriscos for forty years, until 1576, in return for a payment of 40,000 ducats to the Crown, the traditional religious balance in the kingdom of Valencia had been irrevocably altered. A quite vigorous campaign of missionary work and catechism among the Moriscos continued from the late 1520s until their final expulsion in 1609 (see chapter 8), and before this admission of defeat, some of the most enthusiastic and distinguished Spanish churchmen of the sixteenth century applied their brains and energies to the true 'conversion' of the nominally Christian Moriscos. The kingdoms of Granada and Valencia in this period were often explicitly compared to the mission fields of the New World in America. As in Granada in the time of Archbishop Talavera, some friars and priests tried to learn Arabic, and Archbishop Martín de Ayala produced in 1566 a special catechism, in alternating Spanish and Arabic, for educated Moriscos. Generally speaking, however, the Christian missionary effort in both Granada and Valencia in the sixteenth century was more successful in establishing an institutional framework than in converting hearts and minds. It was only in the last decades of the century that the Holy Office became actively involved in the campaign, and by then the radical solution of expelling the Moriscos was near.

As the sixteenth century progressed, the Spanish Inquisition did not have its troubles to seek, and was increasingly forced by economic circumstances to look for new areas of investigation. At the higher political level, the instability which followed Isabella's death, in 1504, put into question the continuing existence of the inquisitorial tribunals. Their many and increasingly vociferous opponents, whether themselves conversos or not, had high hopes that the new king of Castile, the Habsburg Philip I, who was married to Ferdinand and Isabella's eldest surviving child, Joanna (later known as 'La Loca', or 'the Mad') and had been brought up in the Low Countries where there was no Inquisition, would curb the inquisitors' powers, or even abolish the Spanish Inquisition altogether. His death in 1506 put an end to such hopes for many decades, but, as political, economic and social instability continued throughout the Iberian peninsula, one important problem remained. The zealous work which had been carried out by the inquisitors since 1480, together with the royal policy of allowing the sale of exemptions from the tribunals' actions to the wealthier conversos, now threatened to block their main source of income, the confiscation of the goods of those who were accused of Judaising. Given that, as has been noted, inquisitorial action among former Muslims in the Crown of Aragon and in the kingdom of Granada was subject to restriction throughout the sixteenth century, other groups of 'suspects' had to be found, if the Inquisition was not to become bankrupt. Virtually until the end of its existence, real or imagined Judaisers were pursued, and sometimes burned, and converts from Islam were increasingly accused of reverting to their previous, or ancestral, faith. The tribunals' attention, however, was increasingly given, as at the time of its beginnings in the thirteenth century, to dissent within the ranks of the Church itself, among 'Old Christians' as the Spanish jargon of the day had it.

The extent to which the Spanish Church was, or was not, 'reformed' during the sixteenth century remains a subject of deep and often fervent controversy. Most scholars still approach the question either as professing Christians, with their own modern denominational blinkers firmly in place, or as supposedly 'post-Christian' sceptics or atheists, who none the less generally retain either a Catholic or a Protestant bias in their approach to questions concerning Christianity. There are thus two main 'stories' of the Inquisition and the Spanish Church in the period of the Reformation and Counter-Reformation. The traditional Catholic version has seen the Inquisition as the preserver of 'true' Christianity against the infiltration of 'converted' Jews and Muslims, and of Christian dissenters, all of whom falsely claimed to be orthodox members of the Church which, in the words of the Nicene creed, is held to be 'One, Holy, Catholic and Apostolic'. The alternative, Protestant story views the Spanish tribunals as the cruel and arbitrary agents of a godless papistical religion, who suppressed truly godly reformers both within and outside Spain. The confusion which surrounds the relationship between the Inquisition and Judaism, whether in the form of Jews or conversos, is thus fully matched by later treatments of the tribunals' approach to attempts to reform the Church in the sixteenth century. There is still not, and probably never will be, a value-free set of terms to replace such treacherous words and concepts as 'Catholic', 'Evangelical', 'Protestant' or even 'Reform' and 'Reformer', in such discussion, so that they will have to be used here, with due caution. On the face of it, there is little sign of overtly Protestant dissent, in the sense of direct links with outside reforming groups, within Spain in the period between the publication, at Wittenberg on 31 October 1517, of Martin Luther's ninety-five theses on abuses in the sale of papal indulgences and the death of Philip II of Spain on 13 September 1598. In the 1520s, Lutheran and Erasmian books circulated relatively freely in Spain, the latter with the evident approval of Charles V and his entourage. Throughout this period, though, virtually all Spaniards, including the inquisitors, remained extremely vague in their use of terminology concerning the reformers. The term 'Erasmian', from the name of the Dutch humanist Desiderius Erasmus of Rotterdam (1466/9–1536), is a coinage of modern scholars and therefore was not used in the sixteenth century, although energetic Spanish supporters, such as Charles V's Latin secretary Alfonso de Valdés (*c.*1492–1532) would certainly have merited the description. The term *luterano* (Lutheran), from the name of the German former friar (1483–1546), was routinely employed, not least by the Inquisition, throughout the early modern period, to refer to a very much wider range of Christian dissenters. In the latter part of the sixteenth century, it was often used of Calvinists, the followers of the French reformer John Calvin (1509–64), and to refer to members of Elizabeth I's Church of England, which Spanish inquisitors commonly described as 'the new religion' (*la nueva religión*), and which only became known as late as the nineteenth century as Anglicanism.

The attitude of the Spanish Inquisition to institutional and individual attempts to reform the Church, both within and outside Spain, in the sixteenth century was complicated by the pre-existence of reforming tendencies, which had been developing quite steadily during the reigns of Ferdinand and Isabella. Not surprisingly, perhaps, modern scholars have generally been as confused by these phenomena as the inquisitors themselves, not least because of the problems of terminology, combined with hindsight, which have already been referred to. Although the Inquisition of Ferdinand and Isabella was almost totally concerned with rooting out what it perceived to be Judaism in the Spanish Church, the very universality of its requests, repeated in every publication of an edict of grace or faith, that all people should confess every error of Christian doctrine and practice which they knew of in themselves and in others, inevitably threw up a wide range of other material. Little such 'pre-trial' material survives from the early days, but an exception is the register of the tribunal of Soria and Burgo de Osma, for the period between 1486 and 1502. Here, individuals accuse themselves and others of a wide range of words and acts of irreverence towards the Church and its teachings, some apparently caused by ignorance, but others seeming to arise from a materialistic world-view which is today more commonly associated with post-Enlightenment science and philosophy (see chapters 9 and 10) than with the lifetime of Luther, Calvin and Ignatius Loyola. Such evidence commonly failed to reach trial, or else disappeared into the formulaic lists of charges of Judaising which awaited the vast majority of those who faced the Inquisition before 1530. This may help to explain the conspic-uous slowness of the inquisitors, who in the sixteenth century were ever more tightly controlled by the central Council of the Supreme Inquisition (commonly known as 'La Suprema'), to respond to the growing threat posed to

Catholic unity and orthodoxy by the German reformers and their followers elsewhere. Traditionally, attention has mainly focused on academic disputes and achievements. Cardinal Cisneros, who was himself inquisitor-general from 1507 until his death ten years later, also set up his foundation in Alcalá de Henares, the original Complutensian university to the east of Madrid, as a centre of Catholic scholarship which acknowledged many of the achievements of the Italian Renaissance. Its major scholarly achievement was the publication, in 1522, of the 'Polyglot' Bible, which included the text of Scripture in Hebrew, Greek and Chaldean, in columns next to the Latin of St Jerome's Vulgate. Cisneros, who has been for many a symbol of what has come to be called 'Catholic Reform', in other words reform of the Church which avoided separation from the papacy in Rome and worked largely within existing structures. Yet this Cardinal, archbishop, and inquisitor was also a Franciscan friar, who, with the strong support of Isabella and Ferdinand, had fomented reform in many parts of the Church, including the religious orders of monks, nuns and friars, as well as cathedral and parish clergy. It is often forgotten that most, if not all, of the effort made to reform the Western, or Catholic, Church in the sixteenth century, at least up to the end of the General Council of the Roman Church at Trent, in 1563, was predicated on unity and not division, or schism, as it was known in ecclesiastical jargon. In 1525, the trial was begun by the inquisitors of Toledo of a group of Christians, with no obvious Jewish connections, who were associated with the aristocratic Mendoza family, and lived mainly in Guadalajara and Pastrana, east and south-east of Madrid. Their version of Christianity, which they undoubtedly regarded as orthodox, seems to have originated in the very reforming strands of the order of Franciscan friars which had been so much favoured by Cardinal Cisneros. The group, which contained both clergy and lay Christians, was followed by various others during the sixteenth century, and became commonly known by the name of '*alumbrados*' or 'illuminated ones', on account of its practice of various techniques of deep prayer. The Inquisition feared such people because their private devotional life, which was outside the established structures of religious orders and parish life, and their tendency to make exuberant demonstrations during public worship, which in later centuries would have been described as 'charismatic', appeared to threaten the whole organisation of the Church and its conventional devotional life. The Guadalajara and Pastrana groups were eventually condemned by the Inquisition to the relatively light punishments of fines and imprisonment, but the Suprema and the regional tribunals had now been thoroughly alerted to the dangers of unconventional Christian practice not only from foreign Lutherans but also from members of the Spanish Church who were not apparently of Jewish or Moorish origin. In order to counteract this perceived problem within Spain itself, the inquisitors of the reigns of Charles V and Philip II adopted two main strategies, the first being to employ the traditional method of identifying and punishing leading dissidents, and the second being to use the Inquisition increasingly to police both religious and social conformity among the population as a whole, at least partly as a preventative measure.

At the highest religious and academic level, the 'crisis' of inquisitorial activity came in 1559, when Fernando de Valdés, the archbishop of Seville, was inquisitor-general. Philip II had recently become king in succession to his father Charles. He had also returned to Spain, via Flanders, from his brief reign as consort of Mary Tudor, with its unsuccessful attempt to restore Catholicism in England. In that year, the Spanish Inquisition produced its first national 'Index of Forbidden Books', which was not identical with that issued by the Roman Inquisition (see chapter 7), and major trials of supposed Protestant sympathisers in the major economic and political centres of Seville and Valladolid. Also, Bartolomé Carranza (1503–76), a Dominican friar from Navarre, who had been a close adviser of Philip and Mary in England, and had since been appointed as archbishop of Toledo, was arrested and tried by the Holy Office on the grounds that his *Commentary of the Catechism*, which had been published in the Netherlands in 1558, was excessively influenced by the 'heretical' ideas which he had encountered in England. He was to die in Rome, after seventeen years' imprisonment in the care of the Spanish and Roman Inquisitions, and he was not to be the last academic Christian to suffer from the inquisitors' fear of what they called 'Lutheranism', as well as the imagined threat of Judaising. An Augustinian friar, theologian and poet, Luis de León (*c*.1527–91), like Carranza as the result at least in part of an academic and professional quarrel, spent four years under inquisitorial arrest in the 1570s, though unlike the Dominican archbishop he was then able to return to work. At the level of the general public, though, the Spanish Inquisition was mainly experienced, as the sixteenth century progressed, as a police court of morals and suppresser of the unusual – gypsies, witches, Judaisers, crypto-Muslims, Lutherans and, increasingly, bigamists, homosexuals and priests who molested their male or female penitents during the administration of the very sacrament of penance or reconciliation which had led to the setting up of the Inquisition in the first place.

7

THE SPANISH INQUISITION ABROAD

Ferdinand and Isabella's victory in Granada greatly speeded up the process whereby Spain became a European, and then a world, power. Along with other manifestations of Spanish civilisation and culture, the Inquisition was thenceforth to be spread into other spheres of influence, within the Iberian peninsula itself, in Italy, the Netherlands, briefly in England, and also in Spain's American dominions. Between 1580 and 1640, Portugal and its empire came under the Spanish Crown, so that its own inquisitorial tribunals, both in the mother country and in India, were for that period a part of the Spanish Inquisition. Just as the medieval Inquisition had originated outside Spain, so separate tribunals continued to exist in the early modern period, notably in Italy.

Within the Iberian Peninsula: Navarre

The small Pyrenean kingdom of Navarre, on the frontier of Spain and France, was not legally subject to the Spanish Inquisition until 1513, after Ferdinand had effectively annexed it to Castile in the previous year. Nevertheless, Navarre's independence had been restricted ever since it had first been subjected to the Trastamaran dynasty, of which both Ferdinand and Isabella were a part, early in the fifteenth century. In the case of the Inquisition, the Navarrese became involved as a result of the fact that some of those who had conspired to murder the inquisitor of Saragossa, Pedro Arbués, in September 1485, fled to Tudela. From then onwards, the Tudelans put up violent resistance to the Aragonese Inquisition's attempts to retrieve both the suspects in the Arbués case and other conversos who had crossed the border into Navarre to escape interrogation. The stand-off lasted throughout 1486, but in spite of a papal letter issued by Innocent VIII in April 1487, which ordered all Navarrese officials to assist the Aragonese Inquisition in every way, on pain of excommunication, it was only in February 1488 that a compromise was finally reached between the representatives of Tudela and Ferdinand and Isabella. Thus, although there was no separate inquisitorial tribunal in Navarre until after the 1512 annexation, the small kingdom was none the less subject to the ministrations of Aragonese inquisitors and their officials throughout the Catholic Monarchs' intervention. In these circumstances, it is perhaps more surprising that the rulers of Navarre, Catherine and Jean d'Albret, should have initially received numbers of Jewish refugees from Aragon and Castile after the issue of the 1492 expulsion edicts than that the kingdom should have issued its own such edict at the beginning of 1498. By this time, there were few Jews left in Navarre, but the incentive for the inquisitors was the presence of conversos, many of whom had fled from their tribunals in Castile and Aragon. As elsewhere in the

Peninsula, such 'New Christians' remained the main object of the Inquisition's attention until some way into the sixteenth century. Lower Navarre, part of the kingdom to the north of the Pyrenees, remained in the hands of the Albret family, and then passed to the French Crown. Initially, the Inquisition for Spanish Navarre was based in the former seat of resistance to its work, Tudela, although the viceroy and Cortes had requested the establishment of a tribunal in their capital, Pamplona. When the armies of Francis I of France invaded Navarre in 1521, the Tudela inquisitors fled to Calahorra, which was immediately transferred from its former Castilian jurisdiction of Valladolid to cover Navarre as well. In 1570, this tribunal finally settled in Logroño, a central location between its Navarrese and Basque territories. Here it became fully integrated into the work of the Castilian and Aragonese Inquisitions, under the authority of the Suprema in Madrid.

Portugal and Goa

Like the neighbouring Spanish kingdoms, late-medieval Portugal contained a significant Jewish community, which in the late fifteenth century numbered approximately 30,000, or 3 per cent of the total population. In the major towns, especially Lisbon and Oporto, and along the border with Spain, Jews may have numbered up to 10 per cent of the inhabitants. In 1392, at the time when Jews in Castile and Aragon were being subjected to physical attack and increasing legislative pressure, as well as the preaching of Christian missionaries, their Portuguese co-religionaries received renewed protection of their legal and religious status from the new monarchy

An Italian blend of Picart's engraving of burnings by the Inquisition in Lisbon with later representations of penitents in sambenitos.

of the house of Avis. Some Spanish Jews and conversos took advantage of the current Portuguese royal policy and settled in the neighbouring kingdom. Tensions increased when Portugal began to receive converso refugees after the Spanish inquisitors began their work in Andalusia in 1480. The new immigrants brought with them the stigma of being false Christians, and there were soon incidents of violence against them, in Lisbon for example. King John II responded to this disorder by setting up a panel of inquisitors for the kingdom and giving conversos permission to leave it, on condition that they moved to another Christian country. Some convicted

Judaisers were burned in Lisbon and Santarém and, ominously, a small number of native Portuguese Jews were imprisoned for supposedly proselytising among the conversos. In this climate of fear and suspicion, the established Christian population began to blame their Jewish fellow citizens, as well as the Spanish conversos, for the kingdom's problems, including outbreaks of the plague. In addition, Christian preaching was increasingly targeted on the Jews. The difficulties of assimilation reached crisis proportions, however, when thousands of new refugees arrived. It is estimated that at least 20–30,000 Spanish Jews crossed the frontier at this time, and problems soon arose from this virtual doubling of Portugal's Jewish population. A further outbreak of the plague served to increase hostility against the newcomers. The monarchy of John II favoured the settlement at least of the richest immigrants, but at the price of 6,000 *cruzados* for each of 600 families, with lower rates for the rest. The wealthy seem to have been a minority, however, and many of the arrivals from Spain were artisans who threatened to compete with the native population. In addition, as in so many humanitarian crises of this kind, some Spanish Jews avoided the extortionate charges then being levied by customs officials at the border and entered Portugal illegally, thereby acquiring a particular vulnerability. There was still only a rudimentary Inquisition, on the traditional episcopal model, in the kingdom at this time, and, as Jews the new Spanish immigrants were not subject to the ministrations of the normal ecclesiastical courts or the existing inquisitors. However, royal authority was far from providing the majority of the refugees with protection and security. In fact, John II's government took the younger children away from Spanish

Jews who either failed to pay the basic entrance fee of 8 *cruzados* per head or else were illegal immigrants. The unfortunate children were despatched to the island of São Tomé, off the coast of West Africa, to be indoctrinated as Christians and work there in the burgeoning sugar-cane industry. On 19 October 1492, John II issued a law guaranteeing social and fiscal privileges to Spanish Jews who converted, both parents and older children. In order to escape from their effective servitude to the Crown, many responded to the offer by being baptised. The Portuguese king was also considering the issue of his own expulsion order to his Jewish population, both established and immigrant, as early as 1493. Then and in the following year, he made efforts to encourage Jews to convert or emigrate, though wealthy members of the Jewish community continued to help fund the Crown's naval activity. On 25 October 1496, John II died and was succeeded by his brother-in-law Manuel, duke of Beja, who initially put a stop to anti-Jewish violence, and not only guaranteed the Jews' existing privileges but also freed those who had previously remained in royal servitude. The hopes of the Jews were dashed, however, when their expulsion from Portugal became a condition of Manuel's marriage to Isabella, the daughter of her namesake and of Ferdinand. As in the case of Spain, the primary purpose of the edict of 1497 seems to have been conversion rather than expulsion. No specialised Inquisition awaited the converts, however, as they were to be exempted for twenty years after baptism from any investigation of their religious beliefs and practices. Portuguese Christian sources, including the early sixteenth-century humanist chronicler Damião de Gois, report that even without the presence of inquisitors some of the new 'Christians' suffered appalling violence and cruelty. The expulsion edict, dated 5 December 1496, gave Jews a year to leave Portugal (a similar order was made against Muslims), and it was administered by means of officially sponsored deceit on the part of the monarchy rather than the Church. While the Muslims were allowed to leave peacefully in April 1497, ironically with a safe-conduct from Ferdinand and Isabella, the king had no wish to lose the services of his economically active Jews. According to Gois and other chroniclers, Manuel's plan seems to have been that a forcible conversion of Portugal's Jews should take place on Easter Sunday 1497, after the unwilling neophytes had been assembled at Lisbon. Leaks from the Royal Council meant that the execution of the plan was brought forward by a month, to the beginning of the Christian penitential season of Lent. The result was an atrocious and cynical two-part stratagem, worthy of state behaviour in later centuries. First, children were forcibly separated from their parents, on the model which had already been applied in 1494, so as to be taken away and indoctrinated as Christians. Some of the children were murdered by their parents, by suffocation or drowning, to save them from the baptismal font. Others were taken in by 'Old Christians', who took pity on the Jews, but the second part of the royal plan was then put into effect. The adult Jewish population was 'concentrated' in the quarter of the capital, Lisbon, which was known as 'Os Estaos', having been told that they were to board ships to leave Portugal. Instead, they were forcibly baptised, and then received back their children. Thus was created a largely, if not entirely, unwilling 'New Christian' population which, through its descendants, was to provide much business both for the Spanish and for the later Portuguese Inquisitions, as well as strengthening the Sephardic Diaspora in Europe and elsewhere. This is the traditional account based on the chronicles, but archive material suggests that not all the Jews came to Lisbon and that not all of them were baptised. In addition, although the Jews officially had until the end of September 1497 to leave the country, the Crown had already started to confiscate synagogues and their contents before Easter of that year. On 19 March, Palm Sunday, the Sunday before Easter, a number of forced baptisms took place and, subsequently, a deadline of 30 May 1497 was set by the Crown. All Jews who were baptised before that date were pardoned for any crimes which they might have committed previously, while those baptised subsequently were not.

Despite the 'agreement' of 1497, Manuel I asked the papacy to authorise an Inquisition for Portugal as early as 1515, though without success. The king was no doubt influenced by the strong anti-converso feeling which had continued among the majority 'Old Christian' population, and which had already resulted in a violent attack on 'New Christians' in Lisbon at Easter 1506. Manuel's successor, John III, first confirmed the exemption of the conversos (as in Spain, the term referred additionally to the descendants of Jews who had been baptised) from investigation of their Christian orthodoxy, but, after the alarm caused in the kingdom in 1531 by the Jewish messianic movement led by David Reubeni, the king finally obtained the requisite papal bull from Paul III. It was issued on 23 May 1536, and appointed as inquisitors the bishops of Coimbra, Ceuta and Lamego. King John was to be allowed to name a fourth inquisitor from among the bishops, religious, theologians and canon lawyers of the kingdom. It was published in Evora on 22 October 1536, and the first inquisitor-general was the bishop of Ceuta, Diogo da Silva, who was a Franciscan friar and the king's confessor. The first *auto de fe* was held in Lisbon four years later. From the very beginning, the Crown took an active role in the operation of the tribunal. Unlike its Spanish equivalent, the Portuguese Inquisition was never established in the Americas, but although Brazil was thus free of its ministrations, the same could not be said of the 'State of India' ('Estado da India'), which included possessions in Africa as well as in India itself. The colony of Goa became the centre of inquisitorial activity in Asia with the burning in 1543 of a 'New Christian' doctor named Jerónimo Dias, after a hasty episcopal trial. A specialised Inquisition was not set up in Goa until 1560, where it functioned as a check both on Portuguese conversos of Jewish origin and increasingly on converts to Christianity from native Indian religions, until its abolition in 1812.

Outside the Iberian Peninsula: Italy — Sicily and Sardinia

Ferdinand's policies towards Jews and conversos in his mainland Aragonese and Catalan territories were soon applied in his island kingdom of Sicily, which had been Aragonese territory, though far from undisputed, since the thirteenth century. Here and in Sardinia, unlike the case in the rest of Italy, inquisitorial authority derived from Spain and not from Rome, and the focus was on Judaising among 'New Christians'. According to a census undertaken by the island's Jewish council in 1489, there were about 6,300 Jewish households in Sicily, the largest communities being in

Palermo (850) and Messina (400). As in Spain, an expulsion edict was issued on 31 March 1492, but the Sicilian case reveals with stark clarity issues and features which appear more complex and ambiguous in the Iberian peninsula itself. As in Castile and Aragon, a distinct form of edict was drawn up for the island, in this case revealing explicitly the role of Tomás de Torquemada and his Inquisition in the measure. Here, as in other territories of the Crown of Aragon, much of the resistance to the order of expulsion or conversion against Jews came from the leaders of the majority Christian population, and was based on constitutional opposition to the intrusion of a Castilian institution. The edict was issued none the less, and Sicily's Jews were faced with the choice of departure or conversion. In the latter case, they were allowed to retain their property and continue as residents in the island, thus creating a new group of 'judeoconversos', who soon came under suspicion from the Inquisition. As in the case of Portugal, there was no specific Sicilian tribunal for twenty years, but Torquemada and his successors as inquisitors-general, with the king's authority and support, intervened from the start in the affairs of the island kingdom's Jewish Christians. An edict of faith was published in Palermo on 8 November 1500, but it was not until 1511 that the Sicilian Inquisition began its work. By this time, it was widely supposed that Judaising was common, if not universal, among the 'New Christians' and, between 1511 and 1550, no fewer than 1,850 of them were either 'reconciled' to the Church or 'relaxed to the secular arm' for burning. After this, trials of conversos declined to nothing but, in the first half of the sixteenth century, the Sicilian Inquisition provided an example of unparalleled violence to the rest of Italy. In the latter part of the century and thereafter, the tribunal followed the example of its Spanish equivalents in widening its scope to include those accused of Protestantism and other offences of intellect and thought. Anti-Spanish resistance, based on real or supposed constitutional grounds, continued to occur from time to time, and frequently focused on the Inquisition.

The lack of surviving archives makes it hard to assess the activity of the inquisitorial tribunal in Sardinia until the latter part of the sixteenth century, but it is known that an edict for the conversion or expulsion of the island's Jews was issued by the Aragonese chancery on 31 March and that, as in Sicily, inquisitorial action was delayed for twenty years. In the rest of Italy, though, the Roman rather than the Spanish Inquisition was in operation.

The Roman Inquisition

The Inquisition had, of course, originated as a papal institution. By 1263, a cardinal was already acting as inquisitor-general, and a tribunal was operating in Venice, for example, from 1289. Rome continued to be the ultimate authority for all inquisitorial action, even in Spain after 1478, but its authority was also effectively devolved to tribunals in other parts of Western Europe, including Germany and England as well as Italy itself. On 4 July 1542, as a response to the religious turmoil of the two previous decades, Paul III established a new body in the Curia, or papal court, at Rome, which was to be known as the 'Congregation of the Roman and Universal Inquisition' or the 'Congregation of the Holy Office'. The new 'Roman Inquisition', as it was also commonly described, consisted originally of six cardinals, under the leadership of Giovanni Pietro Carafa, who was later Pope Paul IV (1555–9). Carafa's Inquisition attempted to revive, and control, tribunals in other parts of Italy including most notably that of Venice, which in the latter part of the century sat in judgement on the religious beliefs and practice of numerous Spanish and Portuguese Jews and conversos.

Spanish America

As early as 1522, only a year after the capture by Hernán Cortés of the Aztec capital of Tenochtitlan (now Mexico City), the Spanish Inquisition reached the New World of the Americas. Inevitably, part of its work focused on converts from Judaism, who may have travelled to the Antilles (West Indies) and the mainland in order to escape persecution in Spain. On this basis it has sometimes been suggested, without any sound documentary basis, that Christopher Columbus himself was a Jew, and filled his boats with Jews and conversos. In reality, the trial of those deemed to be suspect in Christian orthodoxy included both Spanish conversos and Native Americans, though there was official opposition to including the Native Americans in the Inquisition's remit, and in 1571 Philip II finally removed them to the jurisdiction of the dioceses. After 1580, trials of suspected Judaisers increased in number in Mexico, when Portuguese Jews or New Christians (see chapter 8) began to escape to America from Spanish rule in their home country. In the meantime, since the 1520s, the largely Franciscan mission in the Mexican peninsula of Yucatán had been prosecuting Native Americans who had been baptised as

Christians for relapsing into 'idolatry', that is, their former religion. The basic outlines of the repression of dissident religious belief and practice in Spain's American possessions were thus set for the duration of Spanish rule. The Church undertook a war on two fronts, firstly against heresy among colonists of European origin, who had either arrived directly from Spain or else who came from settler or creole families, and secondly against perceived survivals of indigenous religion among Native Americans. In both Mexico and Peru, traditional European battles between the Inquisition and the main Church hierarchy were refought in the period between the first Spanish conquests in the sixteenth century and 1800. Thus the battle against Judaism in the Catholic Church was combined with campaigns for what was referred to as the 'extirpation of idolatry'. The result was almost continual conflict, throughout this period, between Church and colonists on the one hand, and between the Inquisition and diocesan bishops and their clergy on the other. Generally, the view prevailed among the Spaniards that the teaching of Christianity to the Native American population required much more subtle and all-embracing methods of control than a traditional European Inquisition. Meanwhile, on the other side of the Atlantic, the Spanish version of the Inquisition had become involved with a problem which was much closer to its original context – the rise of Protestantism in northern Europe.

The Netherlands

The Dutch provinces, also known as the Netherlands, became a direct Spanish interest as a result of Charles I of

Castile and Aragon's accession to the thrones of the two kingdoms in 1516. They were part of his inheritance from the dukes of Burgundy, who had been members of the French royal family, the Valois, but had held lands from both the French Crown and the Holy Roman Empire. Many issues were involved in what became known to subsequent centuries as the 'Dutch revolt', but one of them was undoubtedly the question of heresy and its attempted repression. Like all other territories in late medieval Western Europe, the Netherlands had heresy laws, which were administered by ecclesiastical courts in conjunction with the diverse and fragmented secular authorities in the region. When, in 1556, Charles divided his lands, Philip inherited all the Netherlands. This was despite the fact that part of the territory owed allegiance to the Empire, of which Charles's brother Ferdinand was the heir. By this time, with the failure of various attempts at reconciliation between Catholics and Lutherans, to which Charles V had devoted much of his energy and resources, Protestantism had become a major issue in the Netherlands, just as it was in Germany, France and England. The existing episcopal Inquisition in the Netherlands was extremely active between Philip II's accession and 1560, burning dozens of Protestants, both Lutheran and Calvinist. However, it was the rumour that the king intended to introduce the Spanish tribunal to the Low Countries which played a large part in provoking rebellion. In this case, the reputation of the Spanish Inquisition not only preceded it but proved to be an important political factor without even existing in the area concerned. Thus was the 'Black Legend' of Spain created (see chapter 10).

England

Philip's arrival in England, on 20 July 1554, had raised similar fears. He came as the newly created king of Naples and duke of Milan, as heir to the Spanish throne and prospective king consort of England. The reception given by the English public to his entourage was, to say the least, mixed, but it was self-evident from the start that the restoration of the kingdom to its former obedience to Rome was at the top of the agenda for both Mary Tudor and her new husband. Mary's reign has ever since been notorious for the violent repression of the previously legal reformed Church which had been bequeathed by Edward VI. By the time of the Spanish king's departure in 1557, and the queen's death in the following year, nearly 300 people are known to have died. The legal process which brought them to their deaths was not, however, a 'Spanish Inquisition'. Inquisitorial procedures were certainly used, in particular by the zealous Bishop Bonner of London, but they were carried out under parliamentary statute. In January 1555, Parliament restored to the statute book Henry IV's 1401 law 'On the burning of heretics', which had originally been passed to repress the followers of the late fourteenth-century Oxford theologian John Wycliffe (*c.*1330–84). Thus the role of the secular authorities, although crucial in the Spanish case, as well as in Portugal, was even more significant in England. As in the case of the Netherlands, though, Spain's Inquisition was never to be established in this northern kingdom.

8

CONSOLIDATION
AND CRISIS

Perhaps one of the hardest things to understand for those with experience or knowledge of more recent repressive organisations is that during the latter part of the sixteenth century the Spanish Inquisition was generally popular within its own domain. Ferdinand and Isabella's tribunal had excited considerable fear and loathing in its earlier years, both from conversos and from traditionalists who resented its assaults on constitutional practices, especially in the Crown of Aragon. Yet the available evidence suggests that the Inquisition subsequently came to be regarded by most Spaniards with respect if not with love, as a pillar of society. For much of the sixteenth century, although inquisitors became settled rather than itinerant, they continued to undertake regular visitations of their areas, on one occasion or more each year. These visits could take up a large proportion of an inquisitor's time, though, and as time went on they became shorter in tribunals from Toledo to Galicia. It had always been the case, in Spain as well as elsewhere, that the work of the tribunals depended almost totally on the collaboration of the accused and their neighbours. In the sixteenth and seventeenth centuries, the

Inquisition seems largely to have settled into a bureaucratic routine. In general, the local tribunals became less and less free to undertake their own initiatives and increasingly constrained to refer their cases to the Suprema in Madrid for confirmation or decision. This trend has had a considerable effect on the work of modern historians of the Inquisition. The loss of the tribunals' records was considerable, both in the early days of its work before 1500 and more particularly in the turmoil of its end in the early nineteenth century (see chapter 9). This means that when studies are made of the early modern Inquisition in Spain, they very largely depend on the central archive of the Inquisition in Madrid (now housed in the Archivo Histórico Nacional). Material collected by inquisitors before cases were brought to trial is virtually unknown, apart from the register of accusing statements compiled by the tribunal of Soria and Burgo de Osma between 1486 and 1502. Notarial transcripts of the trials themselves exist in much greater numbers, but the main sources for the systematic, and to some extent statistical, study of the Inquisition after around 1540 are the correspondence between local tribunals and the Suprema, and the so-called *relaciones de causas*, or reports on cases tried by the tribunals.

Given the general conservatism both of the Inquisition itself and of its main supporter, the Spanish monarchy, together with the continuing primacy of late medieval inquisitorial manuals such as that of Eymerich, which was amplified and republished by Francisco Peña in Rome in 1578, it is unsurprising that no major innovations took place in the institution's procedures after the early sixteenth century. Yet it would be wrong to conclude from this, as contemporary and later propagandists often did, that the

Inquisition was therefore immovable and monolithic. Even though its basic operational guidelines did not change, both in its practical institutional workings and its targeting of different groups among the population, the organisation constantly evolved and was often remarkably pragmatic, considering the totalitarian nature of its proclaimed purpose and rhetoric. Such pragmatism was manifested in the procedures of accusation, arrest and trial. Local tribunals were empowered to vary the terms of the edicts of faith which they published, or even, as in the case of the Catalan Inquisition after 1580, not to publish such edicts at all. Although, as has been noted (see chapter 6), specialised prison accommodation was built in some places during the sixteenth century, imprisonment remained the fate of the accused rather than the convicted. Thus the Inquisition's prisoners were more likely to spend time in gaol while their case was being investigated than as the result of a sentence, even of 'perpetual imprisonment'. Throughout the early modern period, the inquisitors' prisons, which were still commonly situated in their own headquarters, were frequently, though by no means universally, compared favourably with those run by bishops or the secular authorities. Apart from the secrecy of denunciations and interrogations, the main question on which the Inquisition's more recent opponents have concentrated is that of the use of torture. It should be noted, though, that the 'queen of proofs' was so universal in early modern law courts, both secular and ecclesiastical, that it was not normally in itself a focus of criticism of the Spanish Holy Office until the last decades of its existence. Torture had a respectable pedigree in the history of the Western Church. Jerome (*c*.345–430), the translator of the Latin Vulgate Bible, thought that such torments could and would extract the truth, while both Peter Lombard (*c.*1100–60), whose 'Sentences' or commentaries on Scripture formed the basis of the university curriculum, and Thomas Aquinas (*c.*1225–74) believed that one of the pleasures which awaited the elect in heaven would be to look down upon the tortures of the damned. The instructions issued to inquisitors in 1561 gave no details of the procedure for the administration of torture, but practice indicates that it was only used as a last resort, in a minority of cases. Nevertheless, it was applied to hundreds of people, at least until the middle of the eighteenth century. Torture was used to extract evidence and not as a punishment in itself. As a Church tribunal could not shed blood, the torments were generally administered by a secular executioner, in the presence of the inquisitors, a representative of the local bishop, and a notary to record proceedings. Three main methods of torment were used by the Inquisition. The first, the *garrucha*, consisted of a pulley attached to the ceiling, from which the prisoner was hung with heavy weights attached to his, or her, feet. The torture consisted of raising the accused slowly to the ceiling and letting them fall with a jerk, thus stretching and often dislocating their arms and legs. The second method, known as the *toca*, involved tying the accused down on a rack, keeping his mouth open by force, and pouring water continuously into it through a linen cloth (the *toca*). The third technique, which was most commonly used after 1600, was the *potro*, in which the prisoner was tied to a rack with ropes that were tightened on the orders of the inquisitors. Both men and women were stripped to a few flimsy garments for these procedures, which might be repeated on numerous occasions in order to bring a prisoner to a state of submission. Any attempt to suggest that the Inquisition was 'milder' than contemporary secular tribunals cannot diminish the horror of its tortures, which were administered in all too many cases.

During the sixteenth and seventeenth centuries, as it came increasingly to be seen as a symbol of Imperial Spain, the Inquisition acquired a heraldry of its own, including what would in the late twentieth century be called a 'corporate logo'. This normally consisted of a crest, showing a cross to symbolise Christ's redemption of humanity, an olive branch to represent mercy and a sword, as the instrument of justice and punishment. Often surrounding these emblems were words of Psalm 73, verse 23 (Psalm 74 in Protestant Bibles): 'Arise O God, maintain Thine own cause'. This emblem appeared in places as various as buildings, banners, seals, officials' uniforms, documents, and even inkstands and crockery. Along with this proliferation of the Inquisition's badge came a love for uniformed organisations which was to affect very different denominations of the Church in later centuries. Bands of officials, together with parading confraternities, became features of ever more elaborate *autos de fe*, which were increasingly recorded in visual art as well as printed documentation. Records of the earliest *autos*, whether artistic or written, are rare, and the monarchs normally avoided them, but the later ceremonies were very different. One reason for this was that the role of the familiars (*familiares*) in the work of the Inquisition became much greater as the sixteenth century went on. These were lay officials, who might range in social rank from nobles to artisans, but whose common duty was, at least notionally, to act as the eyes and ears of the inquisitors at times and in places where no official visitation was in progress. The familiars were thus overtly intended to support parish priests and those who confessed their own sins and those of others after hearing the edict of faith, and also to demonstrate to the general population that the Lord would indeed, as the Psalmist had prayed, judge His cause in Spain. In practice, the rank of familiar became a touchstone of acceptability, and of acceptance, for a wide range of Spaniards, and also for their families, who benefited from the fiscal and other privileges which were attached to the office. In particular, it became both a test and a sign of integration into Christian society for those who had ancestors in Judaism or Islam, or who for other reasons had found their way into the records of the Inquisition. A mixture of popularity and necessity thus placed the tribunals at the heart of the Spanish establishment and increasingly made the emblem of cross, olive and sword into a badge of patriotism.

This phenomenon became conspicuous after the religious upheavals of the mid-sixteenth century, during which the division between Catholics and Protestants in Western Europe became permanent, as it still appears at the end of the twentieth century. The trials of 1558–9, including those of the Seville and Valladolid groups and Archbishop Carranza, had effectively eliminated 'native' reforming movements within Spain. Philip II, a self-proclaimed enthusiast for the Inquisition, was clearly disillusioned by the opposition which he had faced in England and the Netherlands between 1554 and 1558, and thereafter fully supported the inquisitors' efforts to prevent Protestant 'contamination' of Spanish territory.

At Court in Madrid, during the early 1560s, rumours abounded that infiltration by German Lutherans, whether real or actual, was threatening to undermine Catholicism in the country at the very time when the final sessions of the Council of Trent (1562–3) were establishing the guidelines for what was to become known as the Counter-Reformation. For the rest of the sixteenth century and well into the next, the Inquisition in mainland Spain continued to arrest, interrogate and punish foreign Lutherans as well as their supposed native supporters. In the Canary Islands, especially after tension with England increased in the 1580s, followers of the 'new religion' of the Church of England received similar treatment. The trials of *luteranos* in Spain do not reveal any systematic attempt to spread the German ex-friar's ideas in the country. Views ascribed to Lutherans during Inquisition proceedings ranged widely, from vegetarianism to support for free love. Such trials rarely focused on the theological issues which had been involved in the trials of the Seville and Valladolid groups, or which had ensnared Archbishop Carranza. It is hard to avoid the conclusion that the Inquisition was used, in the late sixteenth century and at the beginning of the seventeenth, as an instrument to control immigration as well as religious dissidence. This was particularly true after the Calvinist version of Reformed Christianity became widespread in southern and western France in the 1560s. At the level of global strategy, Habsburg policy was permanently preoccupied with the control, and if possible the encircling, of France, and the conflict in that kingdom between Catholicism and Protestantism was seen as a political as well as a religious threat to Spanish Catholic unity. Geography made Navarre and Catalonia the main areas of danger in the eyes of both secular and religious authorities, and the inquisitors in both areas arrested and tried numerous French Protestants in the latter decades of the sixteenth century, while tribunals in Aragon and Castile assisted in the task. In Catalonia in this period, prosecutions of native Protestants were unknown, but, in the early seventeenth century, a new converso group, consisting of converts from Protestantism to Catholicism emerged in the region and became a target of the Inquisition's activity. Suspicion of Frenchmen in general, and of Huguenots (French Protestants) in particular, remained a feature of Spanish life for many decades more.

In addition to its preoccupation with France and Frenchmen, Philip II's Spain was also notable throughout Europe for its leadership of Christian opposition to the spread of Turkish influence on land and sea. The often expressed fear was that the actual Muslim enemy abroad would link up with the potential crypto-Muslim (Morisco) enemy at home, and thus subvert not only Spain but Christendom itself. At the time of the Spanish defeat of the Ottoman fleet during the battle of Lepanto in 1571, the Morisco population of the kingdom of Valencia, and to a much lesser extent those of Aragon, Navarre and Castile, were increasing rapidly, thus increasing fear and paranoia among the Christian majority. The common assumption of all debate concerning the Moriscos in this period was that, although baptised, they were effectively Muslim in their belief and practice. By this stage, the Inquisition was free to target this particular group, though it did not always act entirely in concert with the secular authorities when doing so. Thus while the governmental authorities tended to regard the less numerous and inland Moriscos of Castile, Navarre and Aragon as less of a threat than the much larger coastal populations of Granada and Valencia, the inquisitors were particularly severe in their treatment of the small inland communities. In the years around 1600, the Inquisition's activities, like those of churchmen who were dedicated to the Christian evangelisation of the Moriscos, particularly in Granada and Valencia, were overtaken by the political and religious debate surrounding the perceived threat posed by the continued existence of such groups in Spain. The Turkish threat in the Mediterranean made it self-evident to many that the Moriscos, most of whom despite all efforts remained conspicuously unassimilated to the Catholic Spain of the Counter-Reformation, would have to be expelled. The expulsion of the Moriscos had been proposed to the royal council as early as 1582. On 4 April 1609, during Philip III's reign, such an edict was indeed promulgated, and the Inquisition lost one of its important groups of clients. Over 300,000 people were driven out of the country, and the expulsion seems to have had the characteristics of what has become known in the late twentieth century by the repulsive phrase 'ethnic cleansing'. Nevertheless, because the unfortunate Moriscos had generally been inoffensive and co-operative members of the community, and some of them were conspicuously faithful Christians, the population as a whole did not readily accept official propaganda against them, and much regretted their departure. The first two decades of the seventeenth century were indeed to be a time of crisis and self-questioning for Church and State in Spain.

On the face of it, the removal of Judaisers, Moriscos and Protestants from influence in Spanish society left monarchy and Inquisition as the twin pillars of a uniformly Catholic Christian society, in which the massive programme of evangelisation prescribed by the Council of Trent was being actively pursued. The self-perception of religious and secular leaders in the period of Reformation and Counter-Reformation in sixteenth and seventeenth-century Europe has been all too faithfully absorbed and propagated by many later scholars, who appear to have little personal affection for the Christian faith. These writers thus tend to share with so many Catholic and Protestant reformers of the period the view that much of the population was at best only semi-Christian, especially in rural areas but also among the masses who had migrated to the towns as a result of the economic and social upheavals of the sixteenth century. The terms of the debate, such as 'Christian', 'Catholic', 'Protestant', 'religion' and 'superstition', are rarely defined afresh, so that the inquisitors' own definitions and categories are normally accepted at face value. For the tribunals of Habsburg and Bourbon Spain, as in the days of St Dominic and Pope Gregory IX, the world was basically a wicked place, in which God's faithful, who were uniquely to be found in the Catholic Church that was in obedience to the bishops of Rome, were constantly under attack by diabolical foes, both within and without. At the same time, the Spanish Crown was not only in the toils of battle against Protestant Christians and Muslims, but was also concerned, like other early modern European governments, to police the thoughts and behaviour of its population. In this task, the Inquisition co-operated with a will, pursuing not only religious dissenters but also those accused of moral offences such as male homo-sexuality (sodomy in the vocabulary of the inquisitors), bestiality and bigamy. These were known to lawyers as crimes of 'mixed jurisdiction', because they might be tried by either ecclesiastical or secular courts. In the process of pursuing offenders in these categories, the Inquisition also became a persecutor of Romany, or gypsies. This group, who were generally known to Spaniards as 'Egyptians', seems to have arrived in the country in the early fifteenth century. During the panic over the Muslim revolt in the Alpujarras of Granada in 1499, Ferdinand and Isabella attempted to expel all gypsies who had no lord or employment, but the community has survived in numbers to the present day. After the Inquisition had become a kind of police court for ideas and morals, in the second half of the sixteenth century, the Romany joined other unpopular foreign groups, such as Frenchmen, as ready targets of attack and accusation.

Perhaps most intriguing of all, though, was the Inquisition's attitude and approach to the vexed question of sorcery, magic and witchcraft. It is often stated that the Spanish Inquisition stood out from all other courts and tribunals, whether secular or ecclesiastical, in not taking part in the early modern 'witch craze', in which thousands of people, nearly all women, were burnt or drowned for supposedly harnessing evil forces against others. It is true that an early seventeenth-century inquisitor of the Logroño tribunal, Alonso Salazar y Frías, was instrumental not only in stopping the burning of witches in the Basque country, but also in ensuring that no witch was ever burnt again by the Inquisition. Nevertheless, he had to fight his fellow inquisitor in Logroño to achieve this result, and he was not, in any case, the first to be sceptical about the reality of the apparatus of learned witchcraft theory. In the early days of Ferdinand and Isabella's tribunals, the evidence from Soria and Burgo de Osma shows that some people brought accusations of sorcery (*hechicería*) against others. The accused were all women who were said to have employed love-magic in an attempt to retrieve errant male partners. They were few in number, and there is no evidence that the inquisitors were particularly interested in their cases. This example seems to have been typical of the Inquisition's approach to the question of magic and diabolical possession, which so vexed academic theorists and law-enforcers in early modern Europe. Those who blasphemed against God, and were irreverent towards the Church and its teachings, might expect severe treatment right up to the end of the Inquisition's work in the early nineteenth century. Illicit healers, however, who were generally female, normally experienced stronger opposition from male practitioners in the developing and ambitious medical profession than from the inquisitors. The Sephardic Diaspora, which was the consequence of the expulsion of the Jews from Spain and Portugal, was a matter of very much greater concern to the Holy Office and to the royal government.

Given the apparent decisiveness of royal policy towards Spain's Jews, and the vigour with which Catholic orthodoxy was enforced, it might be supposed that the 'problem' of continuing Jewish belief and practice among Spain's conversos would have disappeared within a generation or two. The fact that this was not the case may be ascribed to events both within and outside the country. The sale by the Crown to conversos of documents that expunged any offences of which they may have been accused by the Inquisition, which had begun before 1500, suggested that there was already a concern at that early stage that Spain would lose by driving out its Jewish Christians. It is not necessary to suppose some kind of specifically Jewish religion (sometimes called Marrano religion, from the term of abuse probably meaning 'swine' which was commonly applied in the period to conversos) in order to understand the continuing prosecution and punishment of Judaisers in Spain in the early modern period: outside influences were also in play. After 1492, Spanish Jews succeeded to a quite extraordinary extent in rooting the language and culture of their home country in their new places of residence, in Italy, Greece, and the Eastern Mediterranean. Yet so often, in the sixteenth century and later, Jews or crypto-Jews in Western Europe are referred to in Gentile Christian sources as 'Portuguese', and by themselves as 'the Nation'. The reason for this link with Portugal, rather than Spain, and for the common confusion among the non-Jewish, or Gentile population as to the religious identity of the conversos, lies in the circumstances of the forced baptism of the majority of Portuguese Jews in 1497. By 1600 'the Nation' had achieved a network which stretched in Europe from Seville and Lisbon in the south to the independent Dutch provinces and the Baltic in the north. The Spanish and Portuguese conversos, who lived sometimes as Catholic Christians in the Iberian peninsula and sometimes openly as Jews in Amsterdam and to a lesser extent Venice, also exploited their native countries' worldwide colonial network in the Americas, Africa, India and the Pacific.

At the beginning of the seventeenth century, and particularly after Don Gaspar de Guzmán, count of Olivares, became chief minister (*valido*) to Philip III in 1622, Spain's earlier treatment of the Jews, as well as the conduct in the matter of Portugal, which was now part of a united Iberian monarchy, became a matter of acute political and intellectual interest. At

least since the latter part of the reigns of Isabella and
Ferdinand, it had been the custom of senior servants of the
royal administration to write memorials of advice to their
masters on matters of government. In the early years of the
seventeenth century, there were two main issues under
discussion: the ever more apparent decline of Spain's
economic and military strength, and the 'purity of blood'
(*limpieza de sangre*) statutes, which excluded individuals of
Jewish or Muslim origin, or else who were descended from
people who had been condemned as heretics by the
Inquisition. Numerous secular and ecclesiastical treatise-
writers now offered two main arguments to those in power.
Firstly, they stated that Spain's decline (in this case including
Portugal's), in relation to the rising power of France, Holland
and England, was to a considerable extent due to the
country's rejection of its able and industrious Jewish citizens.
Secondly, they concluded that the *limpieza de sangre* statutes
were similarly excluding many loyal subjects from the service
of the State. By the end of the sixteenth century these had
spread through many of the main institutions of Spanish and
Portuguese society, including religious orders of chivalry, for
example the Spanish 'military orders' of St James, Calatrava
and Alcántara, and also normal religious orders, cathedral
chapters, university colleges, guilds and confraternities.
Between 1623 and 1641, Olivares, who had a deep conviction
that Spain needed to be modernised, made various attempts
to soften or even remove the statutes, but with little or no
success. In a sense, though, the Count-Duke's zeal was
somewhat misapplied. There had always been grave doubts
about the *limpieza* statutes. They had aroused controversy ever
since conversos were first excluded in 1466 from the service

of the altar of a private chapel in the cathedral, and former mosque, of Córdoba by its founder, the precentor, Fernán Ruiz de Aguayo. As with more modern attempts to exclude individuals from jobs and positions on racial grounds, and in particular the 1935 Nuremberg laws of the Third Reich, it quickly became apparent in Spain that a rigid interpretation of such restrictions on those of Jewish origin would effectively eliminate virtually all candidates. Resistance to the purity statutes came from some religious orders and cathedrals, and from the Inquisition itself, for entirely sound and logical reasons. For if the object of the Christian Church was to bring the whole world to Christ, it was simply not consistent to exclude individuals on the predetermined basis of their racial or religious origins.

The majority of the earliest advocates of the introduction of the new Inquisition to Spain, in the fifteenth century, had been clear that converts were to be tested only on their orthodoxy and not on their previous Jewish lives, let alone their Jewish antecedents. Nevertheless, in the early seventeenth century Olivares was still forced to confront a feeling and prejudice which had already been expressed by one of the most virulent fifteenth-century opponents of heretics in general and Jews in particular, the Franciscan Alonso de Espina (not the later inquisitor of Barcelona, see chapter 3). This was that Judaism, as well as Islam and Christian heresy, were somehow biologically transmitted, and would overcome a person's sincere attempts at true Christian faith and orthodoxy. The influx of conversos from Portugal into Spain, which followed Philip II's annexation of the neighbouring kingdom in 1580, simply highlighted these old and painful issues for both Church and society. The hopes of the

Portuguese immigrants, that the Spanish tribunals would prove less zealous in oppressing them than their newly galvanised Portuguese colleagues, were in most cases demonstrated to be unfounded. The Portuguese immigration, no doubt partly as a result of fears and prejudices which had been aroused by the doings of the Jewish and converso 'Nation' abroad, simply served to breath new life into the Inquisition's pursuit of Judaisers, which continued throughout the seventeenth century. Even later, in the supposedly sceptical eighteenth century, those accused of Jewish belief and practice still constituted the great majority of those tried, for example, by the inquisitors of the Castilian town of Valladolid.

It was only after Bourbons had replaced Habsburgs on the Spanish throne that Olivares's doubts and questionings began to have an effect on the Inquisition and its operations.

9

THE FALL OF THE INQUISITION

In 1700, Spain's Habsburg king, Charles II, was childless and dying, and the two great powers of continental Europe, France and Austria (or the Holy Roman Empire) both had a candidate to offer. The French claim derived from Philip IV's daughter María Teresa, who was married to Louis XIV, while Austria's derived from the marriage of her sister Margarita Teresa to the emperor Leopold. Europe immediately divided on the important issue of who should inherit Spain and its overseas possessions, with William III of England, who spoke for Holland as well, proposing the partition of Spanish territories between the rivals. In the event, Louis's superior strength placed his grandson, who was finally designated as his heir by Charles II, on the Spanish throne as Philip V. The young king arrived in Madrid on a wet day in February 1701, and quickly made a symbolic gesture which was to be important to the future of the Inquisition. He refused to attend an *auto de fe* which the inquisitors proposed to lay on as a traditional welcome to a new sovereign. Philip had to fight for his throne against the Austrians and their allies who included the English, in what became known as the War of the Spanish Succession, which was a worldwide conflict that lasted from 1702 until 1713. Although civil warfare continued after the treaty of Utrecht (11 April 1713), which among its terms gave the Spanish town of Gibraltar to the newly united England and Scotland, because the Catalans favoured the Austrian candidate for the Spanish throne, Archduke Charles. Philip V nevertheless achieved a reign which lasted from 1700 to 1746.

Despite his early decision to avoid attending an *auto de fe*, the first Bourbon king of Spain allowed the Inquisition, exotic and fearsome as it may have been to his Franco-Spanish soul, to function largely as before. Those condemned as Judaisers, Protestants, bigamists or blasphemers continued to be made to process in *autos*, to have the emblems of their shame, their *sambenitos*, hung in their parish churches, or, in the case of men, to be sent to row the king's galleys as slaves, this being a common sentence since the Spanish navy had become over-stretched in the later sixteenth century. Yet the arrival in Spain of the Bourbon dynasty brought a new threat to the institution. The absolutism which had been developed and perfected by Philip's grandfather, Louis XIV, wherever possible brooked no external interference in the affairs of the kingdom. Both he and his successor, Charles III, made it their aim to gain complete control over Spanish ecclesiastical institutions, including the Inquisition. They appear not to have had any intention of abolishing the Suprema and its tribunals, but rather to have aimed to convert it entirely into an instrument of the royal government. This was not so far from the original intention of Ferdinand and Isabella, but in the eighteenth century the Bourbon policy appeared to the inquisitors and their defenders to be a threat to the Catholic faith itself.

1 The Jewish quarter of Seville, and the walls of the Alcázar, or royal castle.

2 The former Jewish quarter of Seville, where attacks began in 1391.

3, 4 Above and opposite:
*The former Jewish quarter of
Seville.*

5 Right: *The former Jewish
quarter of Barcelona.*

7 Hebrew texts on the east wall of the Córdoba synagogue.

8 Moorish arches in the Mosque-Cathedral of Córdoba.

6 Opposite: The cathedral of Barcelona.

NOS EL RECTOR, CONSILIARIOS Y
Colegio mayor de Fonseca de la ciudad de Santiago.

Á los Señores Corregidores, Alcalde mayor, Juez ordinario ó su lugar-Teniente, que jurisdiccion Real ordinaria egerza en

Salud en nuestro Señor Jesucristo.

Hacemos saber, que habiendo provisto el Rey nuestro Señor una Beca vacante en este Colegio mayor de Fonseca, perteneciente á la facultad de
y en atencion á lo prevenido por su Real decreto de arreglo de Colegios, en que manda que preceda, para tomar la posesion, informacion sumaria de cinco testigos examinados de oficio por V. como Juez ordinario de dicho pueblo, donde es natural el Colegial electo, ó lo han sido su Padre y Madre, con asistencia del Procurador síndico general, y ante Escribano Real y público, por la cual se justifique la limpieza de sangre de dicho
Colegial electo; la de sus Padres, Abuelos paternos y maternos, y demas circunstancias que comprenden las preguntas siguientes:

1.ª .... Primeramente, si conoce á dicho Colegial electo, y si es natural de
y á sus Padres, Abuelos paternos y maternos, como se llaman,

ó llamaron unos y otros, y de donde son ó fueron naturales originarios, y si el testigo es pariente, amigo ó enemigo de dicho Colegial electo; si ha sido llamado ó inducido; si le han dado ú ofrecido alguna cosa para que diga en favor ó en contra, y que edad tiene; diga lo que sepa.

2.ª .... Si sabe que dicho Colegial es hijo legítimo, y de legítimo matrimonio de los referidos sus Padres, que lo han educado y criado, y ha sido, y es tenido, y comunmente reputado por tal; diga &c.

3.ª .... Si saben que los Padres del dicho Colegial electo son igualmente hijos legítimos y de legítimos matrimonios, y por tales han sido criados y educados, tenidos y comunmente reputados; diga &c.

4.ª .... Si sabe que, asi dicho Colegial electo, como sus Padres, Abuelos y Bisabuelos por las respectivas líneas han sido y son tenidos, y reputados por Cristianos viejos, sin raza ni mezcla de Judío, Moro ó Converso; y que no han sido condenados, ni penitenciados por el Santo Oficio de la Inquisicion, como Hereges ó sospechosos en la Fé; diga &c.

5.ª .... Si sabe que dicho Colegial electo no es casado, ó desponsado con palabras de presente : que es de vida arreglada y de loables costumbres; que no está infamado de caso grave ó delito feo; diga &c.

6.ª .... Si sabe que del origen ó naturaleza de dicho Colegial electo no hay otro Colegial en el mismo Colegio, ni sabe que alguno de los actuales sea pariente del referido Colegial dentro del cuarto grado de consanguinidad ó afinidad; diga &c.

7.ª .... Si sabe que todo lo que lleva dicho, es público y notorio, pública voz y fama, sin cosa en contrario; y si sabe que á los testigos que han de jurar, ó han jurado, se les da entera fe y crédito en juicio y fuera de él, y por lo mismo se persuade

lines, have been, and are, held and reputed for Old Christians, without race or mixture of Jew, Moor or Converso, and that they have not been condemned, nor given penance by the Holy Office of the Inquisition, as heretics or suspicious in the Faith'.

11 A Toledo inquisitor rested drinks for himself and his friends on this ceramic tray. The sessions, after all, were often long.

12 The synagogue of 'El Tránsito' in Toledo, built by Samuel Halevi in or around 1357. It became a church, dedicated to St Mary, after 1492, and is now a national monument, and the home of the Sephardic Museum.

13 Biblical inscriptions in Hebrew are accompanied by the royal arms of Castile and Léon on the east wall of the 'El Tránsito' synagogue in Toledo. The ensemble of Jewish scripture and Christian royal symbols demonstrates its builder Samuel Halevi's close links with the Castilian Crown.

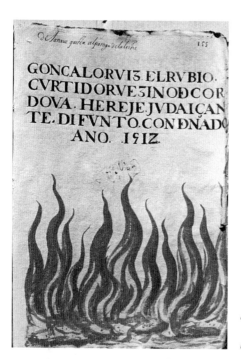

14 *Gonzalo Ruiz 'el Rubio' (Blonde), a tanner, was convicted after death as a 'judaiser' by the Inquisition, and his bones were burnt in 1512.*

15 *Isabel de Herrera, wife of Juan de Bilbao, was 'reconciled' to the Church as a 'judaising' heretic in 1504, when the tyrannical inquisitor Lucero was active in Córdoba.*

16 No-one portrayed more vividly than Goya the distress and shame suffered by Inquisition penitents. In this case, the cross on the sambenito indicates 'reconciliation' to the Church, which still meant humiliation and punishment.

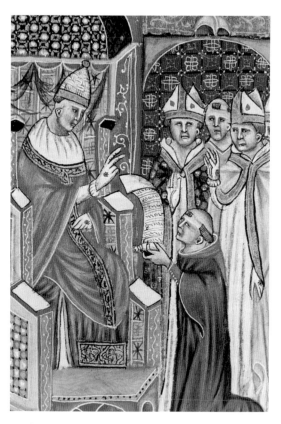

17 Left: *By giving inquisitorial powers to St Dominic (kneeling), Pope Gregory IX set up the 'Holy Office' which was to terrify Europeans for seven centuries.*

18 Below: *An Inquisition scene by Goya. The painter regarded the Holy Office, in its last days, as one of the many horrors and nightmares of a war-torn Spain.*

19 *The Córdoba Alcázar across the site of burnings by the Inquisition, the Campo de los Santos Martires ('Field of Holy Martyrs', named after the nearby Cistercian monastery).*

20 *Part of the royal palace in Barcelona, which housed the tribunal of the Inquisition.*

21 Opposite above: *The medieval city walls of Avila, where Torquemada was prior of the Dominican convent, and those accused of the murder of the 'Holy Child of La Guardia' were tried.*

22 Opposite below: *The Monument to the Cortes of Cadiz, which in 1812 declared that the Inquisition was abolished.*

23 Right: *A fifteenth-century representation of the supposed 'martyrdom' by crucifixion of the 'Holy Child of La Guardia'.*

24 Below right: *Isabella and Ferdinand announcing the expulsion of the Jews in 1492, in the interpretation of Emilio Sala Francés.*

25 Overleaf: *An imaginary version by Pedro Berruguete of a late fifteenth-century* auto de fe, *with St Dominic, whose Order of Preachers supplied many inquisitors, in charge. In reality, all these actions would not have taken place in the same scene. The painter meant to show the terrifying power of the Holy Office.*

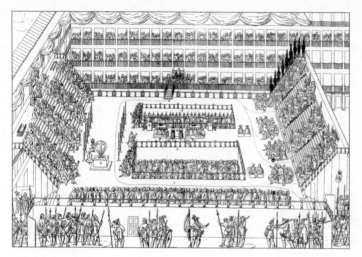

Gregory Fosman: an auto de fe *in Madrid, in the reign of Charles II of Spain.*

Intellectual and political opposition to the Roman Catholic faith also originated in France, and became known as 'the Enlightenment'. By the early years of Charles III's reign, in the 1750s, 'Enlightenment' ideas were beginning to enter Spain and to reach the select band of scholars who were ready to receive them. Thus although in 1759 the Inquisition banned Diderot and D'Alembert's *Encyclopédie*, the measure was no more successful than those taken against foreign books in earlier centuries. Despite the inquisitors' efforts, Montesquieu's ideas on individual freedom, religious toleration and constitutional monarchy also entered Spain, although Rousseau and Voltaire did not achieve the same level of interest and excitement south of the Pyrenees as they did elsewhere in Europe. The reformers who surrounded Charles

III were content to see the Church flourish as a strong support of social order and loyalty to the Crown, but they regarded the Inquisition as a bastion of unfashionable reaction, which was too independent, too deferent to Rome, and too friendly to the now much-hated (and since 1773 officially abolished) Jesuits. From the end of the 1760s, the Council of Castile had reasserted its dominance over the Suprema and its agents. Royal decrees issued in 1768 and 1770 regulated the Inquisition's censorship of books and urged its agents to confine themselves to matters of faith, morals, heresy and apostasy. These were hardly original requirements, and Spanish monarchs had always exerted a strong influence over the tribunals of the Holy Office, but in many ways the efforts of Charles's ministers had limited success. At the highest political level, the late eighteenth-century Inquisition could still threaten the most exalted of them, such as the count of Campomanes, who was highly regarded as an agrarian reformer. Smaller fry, such as the royal intendant of Seville, Pablo de Olavides, found themselves driven out of office by the inquisitors. Olavides was imprisoned for two years, between 1776 and 1778, and then paraded as a penitent in the by then customary indoor *auto de fe*, in this case before an invited audience of nobles, army officers and clergy. A sign of things to come was that Olavides, who seems in reality to have been a moderate Catholic rather than any kind of heretic, then fled to France, whence the nemesis of his prosecutors and judges would soon appear. As late as 1792, another government minister, the count of Floridablanca, used the Inquisition for the Crown's purposes in a vain attempt to censor or exclude radical and revolutionary books from France. This was the essence of the ambiguity of the

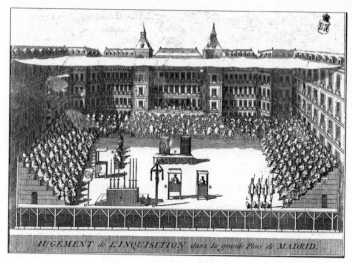

Bernard Picart's engraving of an auto de fe *in the Plaza Mayor in Madrid in 1723.*

Bourbon approach to the tribunal. Its archaic traditionalism could be useful, as long as it was entirely subordinate to the wishes of the Crown. The work of local inquisitors illustrates the point.

Understandably, the strains to which the Spanish Inquisition was subjected throughout the reigns of Philip V and Charles III have suggested to most historians that the institution was in decline in this period. In some respects this is true. In Toledo, for instance, the local tribunal was only hearing three or four cases a year in the later eighteenth century, compared with over 200 in the mid-sixteenth century Of the 4,000 cases referred to the Suprema during the eighteenth century, only 10 per cent involved the major inquisitorial preoccupations of Judaising and Protestantism, a fact which suggests that the tribunals were existing mainly on the more mundane fare of moral and social crimes concerning sex and magic. Only on four occasions in the century, in 1714, 1725, 1763 and 1781, did burnings take place after *autos de fe*. The 1781 death, which was the last such case in Spain, saw the burning alive, as an *ilusa* (visionary), of María de los Dolores López, who had claimed to have direct contact with the Virgin Mary and to have been instrumental in the release of millions of souls from purgatory. This was hardly the way in which the first inquisitors had employed their time during the 1480s. Yet the tribunals seem to have remained active right up to the end of the century, as is shown by that of Valladolid, in Old Castile. In this case, at least, a considerable number of Judaisers and Protestants were tried, as well as soliciting priests who had abused the confessional, bigamists, blasphemers, employers of magic and, in a small number of cases, those accused of being followers of the sixteenth-century '*alumbrado*' movement or of the late seventeenth-century mystic Miguel de Molinos. Contrary to the general view that the Inquisition became more liberal or lax in the eighteenth century, it is clear that torture continued to be used extensively by the Valladolid tribunal, and inquisitors in the 1770s were still worrying that they were not publishing the edict of faith with sufficient frequency. In this case at least, Judaisers, many of them from Portugal, continued to be seen as the main enemy. In Valencia, the inquisitors were the only officials who remained faithful to the Bourbons, when the allies of Austria occupied the city in 1705–7 during the War of Succession. This tribunal actually became economically stronger during the century, thanks to a growth in the Valencian kingdom's population and hence in landlords' income from the enlargement of the cultivated area. Nevertheless, the inquisitors of Valencia, like their colleagues elsewhere, felt the weight of Bourbon insistence that their work should be subordinated to the will of the Crown. In 1790, for example, the government intervened in the case of a Mercedarian friar, Fray Agustín de Cabades, who appears to have been conspicuously guilty of molesting female penitents and conspiring to deceive the Inquisition. His conviction was overthrown as a result of intervention from Madrid, where the Suprema could no longer effectively defend the work of its subordinates. This had not been the only case in which the Valencia inquisitors, like their colleagues elsewhere, felt constrained to suspend or abandon cases which, in earlier centuries, would undoubtedly have been pursued to the end.

The storming of the Bastille, on 14 July 1789, was to change for ever the role of the Inquisition in Spanish society. In Valencia, for example, when war broke out in 1793 between Spain and the new French Republic, the local authorities issued call-up papers to the tribunal's familiars, thus ending one of the last of their privileges. Up until that time, even some of the most 'enlightened' in the city, who were becoming known as 'liberals', were still willing to serve the Inquisition, but the beginning of the French Revolution polarised Spanish society in a new and more violent way. For the king, Charles IV, it was a matter of saving both his own life and that of his cousin, Louis XVI. When the latter aim became impossible, war seemed to be the only course, and the fighting was effectively continuous until the French invaded and overthrew the Spanish monarchy in 1808. In

The French engraver Picart's portrayal of the torture of the accused in an Inquisition prison.

order to meet the cost of the war, the government adopted various financial expedients which included the selling off, from 1797, of entailed properties which had belonged to various public corporations, including the Inquisition. On 27 February 1799, a royal order was issued for the sale by auction of all the immovable property of local tribunals, and the measure was duly put into effect by the Suprema in the following month. The loss of this painfully acquired property ended the fiscal independence of the Inquisition, and paved the way for its abolition, which was not to be long delayed. In August 1805, inventories of the movable goods of the tribunals were demanded by the Suprema, on royal orders, and some valuable paintings thus found their way into the collection of the royal favourite, Manuel Godoy. In 1808, after his fall from grace, and on the orders of the new king Ferdinand VII, the goods concerned were not returned to their previous owners but sold at public auction. Ferdinand had come to power as a result of the abdication of his father, on 19 March 1808. Charles subsequently protested that he had ceded the throne under coercion, and both he and his son were summoned across the French border to meet Napoleon. From the Spanish point of view, the meeting was less successful than that held at Hendaye, on 23 October 1940, between General Francisco Franco and Adolf Hitler. Both Charles and his son were forced to abdicate, and hand the Spanish Crown to Napoleon. On 2 May 1808, the famous 'dos de mayo', the bloody aftermath of which was portrayed by Goya, the population of Madrid rose in rebellion against the French occupation force, which was commanded by Field Marshal Murat. Soon afterwards, Napoleon summoned his brother Joseph from Naples and placed him on the Spanish throne. An assembly of pro-French Spaniards (*afrancesados*) met across the border in Bayonne and acknowledged Joseph as king, but most of the population resisted. Thus began the long, bloody and devastating conflict, known to the British as the Peninsular War and to Spaniards as the War of Independence, which eventually drove the French from Spain, and also gave the world the concept of 'guerrilla' warfare ('little war' in Spanish).

Initially, the Suprema appeared to be generally supportive of the French-backed regime. After the Madrid rebellion had been violently suppressed, local inquisitorial tribunals were reproved for showing support for independent Spanish resistance, and instructed to use their commissioners and familiars to encourage tranquillity and acceptance of the rule of King Joseph. At this stage, there was no hint that the Inquisition was to be abolished. Instead, in tune with Napoleonic France's own return to religion after the atheistic and pagan excesses of the Revolutionary period, the Council of the Inquisition declared that Catholicism was to remain the only religion in Spain and her empire. Inquisitors in the regions were still evidently influenced by local sentiment. For instance, on 26 August 1808, the tribunal of Llerena, in Extremadura, issued a statement condemning the Suprema for its pro-French stance. By this time, however, the French authorities were increasingly interfering in the Inquisition's activities, especially in Madrid. On 28 September, the Suprema announced in protest that it had changed sides, urging all its provincial tribunals to support the Junta Central, which was now co-ordinating Spanish resistance to the French. In Valencia, for instance, the inquisitors responded actively to an order from the Junta, via the Suprema, to ban Masonic activity and seize imports of the writings of Freemasons. Such behaviour merely increased tensions between the Holy Office and the French authorities. Finally, on 4 December 1808, Napoleon himself arrived in Chamartín, then some distance north of Madrid, and issued various decrees. One of them suppressed the Inquisition and all its tribunals, on the grounds that they were a threat to the civil authorities. The moderate and, in the eyes of some, heretical Inquisitor-general, Ramón Josef de Arce y Reynoso, resigned. The Junta Central tried to have the bishop of Orense appointed to succeed him, but the state of war in Europe made it impossible to obtain the necessary ratification from Pope Pius VII (reigned 1800–23). In some places,

An anonymous French engraving of public burnings following an auto de fe.

though, the work of the Inquisition had already been disrupted well before its abolition by the French-backed regime.

Córdoba, for instance, was invaded by Napoleonic troops on 7 June 1808. The royal castle, which had been the Inquisition's headquarters since the 1480s, was ransacked and part of the tribunal's archive was said to have blown away down the Guadalquivir, while some of it was rescued and deposited in the library of the nearby bishop's palace. A more systematic destruction of the Inquisition's records was undertaken early in 1810 by a royal commission. The work was reported to the central government as complete on 11 May 1810. During the political comings and goings of the next few years in Spain, the fate of the Inquisition hung in the balance, being dependent on the success or otherwise of resistance to the French occupation. During the latter part of 1810 and early in 1811, there was some discussion in the Council of Regency, which acted on behalf of Ferdinand, of re-establishing the Holy Office in defiance of the French. In the event, the decision rested with the Cortes, or Spanish parliament, which had assembled, in territory outside French control at Cádiz, on 24 September 1810. At once, a pamphlet war broke out, on the subject of the Inquisition, between the 'conservatives', who saw its defence of Catholic orthodoxy as an essential part of the defence of Spain's identity against foreign aggression, and the 'liberals', who saw the tribunals as an obstacle to progress and freedom. The matter was referred by the deputies to the Committee on the Constitution which they had set up, and its conclusion was that the Inquisition was incompatible with the new constitution. On 22 January 1812, the Cortes agreed, by 90 votes to 60, to end the organ-isation's life, but, in the chaotic circumstances of the period, things were not to be that simple. In the event, despite the efforts of the liberals and progressives assembled at Cádiz, the Inquisition did not disappear from Spanish life, but simply reverted to its traditional medieval form. On 26 January 1813, the relevant passage of Alfonso X's thirteenth-century legal code, the *Siete Partidas*, was restored, giving jurisdiction over heresy cases back to bishops and their deputies (vicars). Of course, this provision applied only to those parts of Spain which were not under French control. In Valencia, for example, which had been captured by Marshal Suchet on 8 January 1812, the Inquisition remained entirely abolished. Meanwhile, on 22 February 1813, the Cortes of Cádiz issued an edict, which was to be read in all parish churches. It explained that the tribunal was an obstacle to Catholic purity, because of its abuses, and that religious orthodoxy would be better preserved by the bishops. The mainly liberal Cortes was by now extremely unpopular in traditionalist circles, and when Napoleon's defeat allowed Ferdinand to return to Spain, on 4 May 1814 he declared all the parliament's acts null and void, and on 21 July of that year he fully restored the Inquisition. In further edicts of 18 August and 3 September, he ordered the tribunals' immovable property, rent income and cathedral canonries or prebends to be restored by the central government. A new inquisitor-general, Francisco Javier de Meir y Campillo, was appointed, and local tribunals at once set to work to recruit new theological advisers (*calificadores*) and familiars.

Like a dying wasp, the restored Inquisition attempted to sting all its enemies before itself departing. In Lent 1815, a new edict of faith was published in Madrid, which not only addressed the old enemies of Judaism, Islam and Protestantism, but also called upon the faithful to denounce those who had become involved with modern rationalist philosophy. Soon afterwards, confessors were instructed once again to refuse absolution to penitents who had not provided a written statement of any doctrinal errors of which they were guilty. Nevertheless, in the turbulent period of the restoration of Ferdinand VII, the Inquisition never regained its former vigour. It suffered economically from the agrarian decline of 1817–8, and was subjected to numerous incidents of local defiance and resistance. Early in 1820, political and social pressure, together with the growing economic difficulties of the post-war period, forced Ferdinand to restore the 1813 constitution, and thus to abolish the Inquisition for a second time. Once again, the tribunals' property was

Goya shows the humiliating procession of a convicted prisoner, wearing a sambenito *and escorted by Inquisition familiars and a hostile crowd, probably to his death.*

Goya shows a convicted penitent at an auto de fe, *listening either to a sermon or possibly to the reading of his sentence.*

confiscated and auctioned, under an order issued by the new Cortes, dated 9 August 1820. In Valencia, at least, such sales had already begun before that date. The liberal government which had forced these measures on the king proved to be so incompetent that a 'liberating' French army, under the command of the duke of Angoulême, was, in contrast to its Napoleonic predecessor, welcomed into the country in April 1823. Ferdinand immediately rescinded all his governmental acts since 7 March 1820, but although this should have meant a further life for the Inquisition, its activity was fitful throughout the rest of the decade. Foreign pressure on the king not to restore the Holy Office was considerable, and his political and financial dependence on France made it effectively impossible for him to resist it. Also, as a result of the turmoil of the previous twenty years, the Inquisition had become a symbol of identity and faith for those Spaniards who had even more conservative views than did Ferdinand himself. In some dioceses, anti-modernist *Juntas de fe* were established, which were against most things that were happening in the modern world, and which targeted the king's supporters as well as liberals. The leader of the Valencian Junta, Dr Miguel Toranzo, had the privilege of pronouncing the last death sentence for heresy in Spain, in 1824, against a schoolmaster from Rusafa called Cayetano Ripoll. The unfortunate teacher had become a deist while in a French prison during the Peninsular War, and refused to recant despite two years' imprisonment and the efforts of numerous Catholic theologians. He was turned over to the secular Audiencia (High Court) of Valencia, and executed on 26 July 1826. As an indication of the growing right-wing tendencies of traditionalist Catholics in this period, the archbishop of Valencia, Simón López, congratulated Dr Toranzo on his efforts in the case. However, the *Juntas de fe* lasted no longer than the following year, and in 1829, at the request of Ferdinand himself, Pope Pius VIII, in what must be regarded as the most notable and historic act of his twenty-month reign, ended over 300 years of almost total effective independence from Rome for the Spanish Inquisition by henceforth reserving all heresy cases in Spain to the jurisdiction of his own tribunal in the Curia. The relevant papal brief was confirmed by Ferdinand on 6 February 1830. As the papal nuncio had indicated when the Cortes attempted to abolish the Inquisition in 1812–3, only the pope could finish what the pope had begun. Yet, as on so many occasions in the reigns of Ferdinand and Isabella, the Spanish Crown had the last word. By an elegant irony, the Inquisition's own property, which its receivers had confiscated from its prisoners, was now handed over to another 'receiver of confiscated goods', this time working for the royal Bureau de Espolios y Vacantes (Office of Spoils and Vacancies). As inquisitors struggled to provide for the surviving retainers of a moribund institution – the commissioners, the familiars – the last act arrived. On 15 July 1834, Ferdinand VII's widow, Queen María Cristina, acting as regent on behalf of the young Isabella II, finally abolished and suppressed the Spanish Inquisition. With appealing symmetry, a second Isabella finished what the first had begun.

10

THE INQUISITION TODAY
IN REALITY AND MYTH

Although the final curtain came down on the Spanish Inquisition in 1834, this certainly did not mean that the Roman Catholic Church had abandoned its defence of Christian orthodoxy, in Spain or elsewhere. On the contrary, the nineteenth and twentieth centuries were to see continuing practical and intellectual efforts by successive popes to counteract what they regarded as tendencies in the modern world which threatened the Christian faith as they believed it to have been handed down from Christ and the apostles. Having faced down, in Napoleon, its greatest direct threat since troops claiming allegiance to the Emperor Charles V had sacked Rome and taken Pope Clement VII captive in 1527, the papacy was forced to confront what it saw as a Hydra-headed monster of opposition thereafter. It was in Spain that the modern distinction between 'liberal' and 'conservative', which the opera librettist W.S. Gilbert (1836–1911) humorously proposed as the only options possible for a baby boy in Victorian England, was first coined. But while this may have been a relatively harmless distinction in the context of the parliamentary debates of the

An early lurid protrayal of Protestant tortures, supposedly carried out at night, from Cavallerius (Rome, 1584).

largely secure ruling class of the expanding British Empire, the same could not be said for the Lords' and Commons' predecessors and contemporaries in Continental Europe. In Spain, the terms represented a violent intellectual and political conflict, which ran through the country's history up to the end of the twentieth century. Although the abolition of the Spanish Inquisition in 1834, like its original introduction to Castile in 1478, legally originated with the papacy, the Inquisition in Rome itself, which was the ultimate repository of Catholic doctrinal orthodoxy, did not disappear at that time. Throughout the nineteenth century, and well into the twentieth, successive popes battled not only for their political independence, against first Napoleon and later the post-1870 unified Italian state, but also against the philosophies and political ideologies of the modern world – liberalism, socialism, communism, and scientific method and research. In 1588, the year of Philip II's Spanish Armada against England, Pope Sixtus V had reorganised Paul IV's Roman Inquisition of 1542. In 1908, to assist in his battle against 'modernism', in other words the influence of the intellectual techniques of the period on theology and Biblical criticism, Pius X (reigned 1903–14) included the Inquisition in his re-organisation of the various congregations, or departments of the Curia in the Vatican, with the title 'Congregation of the Holy Office'. In 1965, Paul VI (reigned 1963–78) reformed the institution as the 'Congregation for the Doctrine of the Faith'. Its function of safeguarding the doctrine of the Roman Catholic Church in faith and morals was augmented at this time by the additional duty of actively promoting sound teaching in the Church. The head of the CDF, as it is commonly known in the Vatican and elsewhere (though it is said that the old name of Holy Office is still used informally) has been, since 1968, a cardinal prefect, like those in charge of the other 'congregations'. The holder of this office since 1981 has been Cardinal Joseph Ratzinger, who has been active in both the roles set down by Paul VI in 1968. Under his leadership, and in close conjunction with Pope John Paul II, the CDF continues, in its traditional inquisitorial role, to vet for doctrinal correctness all major documents which are issued by the Vatican. It also calls in for review, from time to time, the writings of notable Catholic theologians, including Gustavo Gutiérrez, Leonardo Boff and Hans Küng, who have been accused by some of deviating from Catholic orthodoxy. Sometimes, individuals are deprived, in secret proceedings, of their licence to teach Catholic theology, while in other cases they are 'silenced' for a period, while they correct their views, and are then allowed to teach once more as authorised representatives of the Roman Catholic Church. The modern 'Inquisition's' procedures perhaps inevitably betray some influence from the past, especially in their secretive nature, which is explicitly intended to protect the reputation of the innocent, but Cardinal Ratzinger's Congregation cannot resort to the secular arm to enforce its will. In general, those who find themselves directly subject to its ministrations are not taken from the ranks of the ordinary faithful, the 'people of God', as the documents of the Second Vatican Council (1962–5) have it, but are theologians and teachers, in some cases in orders as bishops or priests. Yet, the Congregation for the Doctrine of the Faith does directly reach the whole body of the Church through its vital role in the composition of the *Catechism of the Catholic Church*, which was issued as a result of a decision of an extraordinary synod of bishops, held in 1985.

Although the traditional concern of the leadership of the Roman Catholic Church to ensure that its members receive pure doctrine and teaching has survived bombardment by an apparently infinite diversity of philosophies and religions, which is a feature of the contemporary world, the papacy of John Paul II has also attempted to address some past wrongs. This was especially the case as the two thousandth anniversary of the birth of Jesus Christ (in traditional chronology, at least) approached. In 1992, the pope admitted that the Roman Church had been wrong to condemn Galileo in 1643 for saying that the earth orbits the sun. Another issue

PORTRAITS DE·3·HOMMES CONDAMNÉES PAR L'INQUISITION D'EPAGNE

1 Habit de celuy qui doit estre Brulé vif .
2 Habit de celuy qui a euité destre Brulé en auouant auant que
d'estre jugé .
3 Habit de celuy qui a euité le feu en auouant apres son jugement . voyez t.2.pag.22

Three men in sambenitos *(after Limborch). Such pictures became the common currency of propaganda against the Inquisition in the eighteenth and early nineteenth centuries.*

which has preoccupied John Paul II throughout his pontificate is the often sordid and violent history of the Catholic Church's relations with the Jews. Some non-Catholic Churches, including those in Germany and Austria, have made parallel efforts since 1945 to admit and repent of the part played by their predecessors in fomenting anti-Jewish attitudes among their members, which helped set the scene for Adolf Hitler's attempt to wipe the Jewish people from the face of the earth in the Holocaust. Yet the history of Catholic attitudes towards the Jews goes back much further, and lies at the root of many anti-Jewish phenomena, including the medieval and early modern Inquisition, in Spain as well as much of the rest of Western Europe. It is thus of great significance that the Roman Church under the leadership of John Paul II has made concrete efforts both to alter its teaching on the relationship between Christianity and Judaism, and to admit past wrongs in its treatment of Jews. The process began at the end of the Second Vatican Council in 1965, with the issue of a document on the relation between the Church and non-Christian religions, entitled *Nostra Aetate* (In our age). Ten years later, in January 1975, and still in the pontificate of Paul VI, a comprehensive set of guidelines was issued by the Vatican for the interpretation in practice of the sections of *Nostra Aetate* which applied to Jews and Judaism. In 1985, as a result of the initiative of John Paul II, a further set of notes was published to aid Catholic teachers and catechists in interpreting and applying the Church's renewed and altered understanding of Jews and Judaism. As the jubilee year of 2000 approached, the pope and Vatican attempted to address various unresolved issues from the past, which have shown the Church in a bad light to many. A theological commission, set up by the pope, drafted an apology for the atrocities committed during the medieval Crusades, and finally, the matter of the Inquisition, which is evidently of the utmost concern in Jewish-Christian relations, was addressed in 1998. It was announced that the 'secret' (more 'private' than 'secret' in Italian) archive of the Roman Inquisition would be opened to scholarly research. The archive concerned was built by Pope Paul V in 1610, but, just as the records of the Spanish tribunals suffered severe losses during the Napoleonic period, so the Roman archive was depleted by about a third after it was transported to France in 1809. In 1998, a group of historians was invited to the Vatican to debate the meaning and significance of the records of the Roman Inquisition. Documents dated 1903 or later are still not available for consultation, and there has so far been no 'apology', as such, for the work of the Inquisition.

In Spain, things have proceeded somewhat differently. The battle between conservatism and liberalism, in the midst of which the Spanish tribunals were wound up in 1834, and their property confiscated by the State, developed during the twentieth century into a struggle for the identity of the country that led to a violent civil war and thirty-six years of dictatorship. Under the constitutional monarchy of Juan Carlos I, it has become possible for the State to make an apology for the country's past treatment of the Jews, and of Muslims and Protestants, who now all have their religious freedom guaranteed under the constitution. In 1992, the king made a statement to this effect at the Alhambra, the former Nasrid palace in Granada, in the presence of adherents of the three faiths of Abraham. Today, the Museo Sefardí (Sephardic Museum) in Toledo, sited in the fourteenth-century synagogue built by Samuel ha-Levi, and still known by its post-expulsion Christian dedication of 'El Tránsito', commemorates the role of Jews in Spanish life over two millennia. But if the Inquisition lives on today, it is not only in the memorabilia of the Toledo museum – an inkstand, a seal, a glasses-tray – but also in the minds of those who have been influenced by the work of literary and visual artists.

The actual term *Leyenda negra* ('Black Legend') was coined as late as 1913, by a civil servant in the Spanish Ministry of Education called Julián Juderías. In that year, Juderías (literally

'Jewries') won a prize in a literary competition for a book entitled *La Leyenda negra y la verdad histórica* (The Black Legend and historical truth), which was published simply as *La Leyenda negra*. In it, the author defined the concept as the sum of the fantastic reports about doings in Spain which circulated abroad. At the time, his country was particularly sensitive to foreign opinion, having recently lost, in 1898, its last major imperial possessions, Cuba and the Philippines, to the Americans. Since 1913, the term Black Legend has achieved great popularity among both detractors and defenders of Spain. Yet the origins of this subject are to be found centuries earlier, at the very time when Spain emerged as a power in Western European politics, after the conquest of Granada. The successes of Spanish arms, in Sicily, Sardinia and mainland Italy, aroused both fear and jealousy among the Italians. After the French invasion of 1494, the Italian peninsula suffered a series of violent foreign interventions, by France, Spain, the Holy Roman Empire and the Swiss Confederation, which largely extinguished its political independence. Yet Italians still felt a huge cultural superiority over the foreign invaders and, frequently, rulers, because of the achievements of the Renaissance. From around 1500, therefore, the myth was spread of Spaniards as obsessed with nobility (*hidalguía*), haughty, snobbish and at the same time brutish and uncultured. The Inquisition quickly became associated in Italian minds with this anti-Spanish feeling. When Ferdinand added Naples to his historic domains in Sardinia and Sicily, he attempted to introduce the Spanish version of the Inquisition there, to replace the traditional episcopal tribunal which already existed. The attempt was unsuccessful, and there were further revolts against Spanish rule in Sicily in

1511 and 1526, supposedly against the excesses of Inquisition familiars, and in 1547 and 1564 in Naples, against mere rumours that a Spanish version of the Holy Office was about to be introduced. At this time, a similar rumour helped to precipitate the rebellion in the Netherlands which eventually resulted in the establishment of the independent Dutch Republic.

The growing split between Catholic and Reformed Europe placed Spain on the front line against the Protestant activity of England and the Netherlands. Thus a large addition to the written and visual material concerning the real or supposed atrocities of the Spaniards was provided by Dutch and English Protestants, who saw the country's soldiers and ecclesiastics in action during the reign of Mary Tudor in England, and the attempted repression of revolt in the Netherlands. Both at the time and afterwards, Mary's 'bloody' reputation was inseparably linked to Spain, and to her Spanish husband. France was another important source of anti-Spanish sentiment, and, in the late seventeenth and eighteenth centuries, provided much visual evidence of the atrocities of the Spanish and Portuguese Inquisitions. It is thus hardly surprising that, both during its actual existence and after its abolition, the Holy Office was so often a focus of Spanish identity, for better or worse. In the early seventeenth century, the Count-Duke of Olivares had included a review of the working of the Inquisition and of the 'purity of blood' statutes in his agenda for reforming the government of Spain and its empire. Later, in the crises of the Napoleonic period and the loss of much that remained of the empire in 1898, Ferdinand and Torquemada's creation continued to be treated with almost obsessive intensity. It is good that the record of the Spanish Inquisition should, as far as possible, be set straight. Nevertheless, as long as human beings, whatever their nation and ideology, continue to create victims while they believe they are working for the good, it will be necessary to be vigilant against further 'inquisitions' or their equivalents.

PICTURE CREDITS

GLOSSARY

Most terms are explained in the text, but the following may require further definition.

Anti-pope	A holder of the papal office whose election was eventually declared to be illegitimate
Bachelor	In Spain, a holder of a university bachelor's degree in arts (BA)
Baptism	Ceremony of initiation into the Christian Church
Barbarian	Roman term for the tribes which invaded its empire and established successor states
Caliph	Leader of the Islamic faithful
Choir services	Daily worship held by clergy, sometimes with singers, in cathedrals and other larger churches

Curia	The court of a ruler, in this case that of the bishop of Rome, or pope
Eucharist	Literally 'thanksgiving': a service, involving the consecration of bread and wine, which was instituted by Jesus, at the 'Last Supper' on the eve of his betrayal, and is still central to the life of most Christian churches. Also known as the 'Lord's Supper', the 'Holy Communion', and the 'Mass'
Jeronymite	A member of the late medieval order of friars in Spain and Portugal, which took its inspiration from St Jerome
Legatine	Adjective from 'legate', in this case a churchman given delegated powers by the pope
Mercedarian	Member of a Spanish order of friars, dedicated to the ransoming of Christian captives from Muslim hands
Nuncio	Literally 'messenger', in this case with a specific commission from the pope to transact business in a particular part of the Church
Passion	The sufferings of Jesus in his trial and death

Provincial	The elected head of a provincial area of a religious order of monks or friars
Purgatory	In traditional Catholic theology, a place of trial and torment for the souls of the dead, who await eventual despatch to Heaven
Sacrament	A major Christian service in which a spiritual meaning is symbolised by the use of the material, for example water in baptism and bread and wine in the Eucharist
Sambenito	Robe worn by convicted prisoners of the Inquisition, during an *auto de fe*, and later hung in their respective parish churches
Secular	In the Catholic church, a member of the clergy who is not also a member of a religious order
Succoth	The Jewish feast of Tabernacles, to be commemorated under an open sky

SELECTED FURTHER
READING

The following works have been used extensively, though far from exclusively, in the preparation and writing of this book. They also enable the reader to explore more fully the issues which have been raised here. Figures in square brackets denote the specific chapters for which each reference is of particular use.

Amiel, Charles and Lima, Anne (ed. and trans.), 1997. *L'Inquisition de Goa. La relation de Charles Dellou (1687)*, Paris: Éditions Chandeigne. [7]

Azcona, Tarsicio de, 1964. *Isabel la Católica. Estudio crítico de su vida y de su reinado*, Madrid: Biblioteca de Autores Cristianos. [4]

Azcona, Tarsicio de, 1998. *Juana de Castilla, mal llamada 'la Beltraneja', 1462–1530*, Madrid: Fundación Universitaria Español. [4]

Baer, Yitzhak, [1961, 1966] 1992. *A history of the Jews in Christian Spain*, two volumes, Philadelphia and Jerusalem: Jewish Publication Society. [5]

Barber, Malcolm, 1992. *The two cities. Medieval Europe, 1050–1320*, London: Routledge. [2]

Bartlett, Robert, 1994. *The making of Europe. Conquest, colonisation and cultural change*, London: Penguin Books. [1, 5]

Beinart, Haim, 1981. *Conversos on trial. The Inquisition in Ciudad Real*, Jerusalem: The Magnes Press. [4, 5]

Beinart, Haim, 1985. 'La Inquisición española y la expulsión de los judíos de Andalucía', in *Jews and conversos. Studies in society and the Inquisition*, ed. Yosef Kaplan, Jerusalem: The Magnes Press, pp. 103–123. [6]

Belenguer, Ernest, 1999. *Fernando el Católico. Un monarca decisivo en las encrucijadas de su época*, Barcelona: Ediciones Península. [6]

Benito Ruano, Eloy, 1998. 'Reinserción temprana de judíos expulsos en la sociedad española', in *Pensamiento medieval hispano. Homenaje a Horacio Santiago-Otero*, ed. José María Soto Rábanas, Madrid: Consejo Superior de Investigaciones Científicas. [6]

Bernáldez, Andrés, 1962. *Memorias de los Reyes Católicos*, ed. Manuel Gómez-Moreno and Juan de Mata Carriazo, Madrid: Consejo Superior de Investigaciones Científicas. [6]

Bethencourt, Francisco, 1995. *L'Inquisition à l'époque moderne. Espagne, Portugal, Italie, XVe–XIXe siècle*, Paris: Fayard. [7, 8, 9]

Biget, Jean Louis, 1998. ' "Les Albigeois": remarques sur une dénomination', in *Inventer l'hérésie? Discours polémiques et pouvoirs avant l'Inquisition*, pp. 219–255. [See Zerner] [2]

Biller, Peter, and Hudson, Anne, (eds) 1994. *Heresy and literacy, 1000–1530*, Cambridge: Cambridge University Press. [1, 2]

Cantera Burgos, Francisco, [1944] 1972. 'Fernando del Pulgar and the conversos', in *Spain in the fifteenth century, 1369–1516. Essays and extracts by historians of Spain*, ed. Roger Highfield, London: Macmillan, pp. 296–353. [5]

Cervantes, Fernando 1994. *The Devil in the New World. The impact of diabolism in New Spain*, New Haven and London: Yale University Press. [7]

Clanchy, M.T., [1979] 1993. *From memory to written record. England, 1066–1307*, Oxford, Blackwell. [1]

Cohen, Jeremy, 1982. *The friars and the Jews. The evolution of medieval anti-Judaism*, Ithaca and London: Cornell University Press. [3]

Collins, Roger, 1983. *Early medieval Spain. Unity in diversity, 400–1000*, London: Macmillan. [3]

Conde y Delgado de Molino, Rafael, 1991. *La expulsión de los judíos de la Corona de Aragón. Documentos para su estudio* [=*Fuentes Históricos Aragoneses*, 19], Saragossa: Instituto Fernando el Católico [CSIC]. [6]

Constable, Olivia Remie (ed.), 1997. *Medieval Iberia. Readings from Christian, Muslim, and Jewish sources*, Philadelphia: University of Pennsylvania Press. [3]

Coronas Tejada, Luis, 1988. *Conversos and Inquisition in Jaén*, Jerusalem: The Magnes Press. [4]

Dedieu, Jean-Pierre, 1989. *L'administration de la foi. L'Inquisition de Tolède, XVIe–XVIIIe siècle*, Madrid: Casa de Velázquez. [8]

Dillard, Heath, 1984. *Daughters of the Reconquest. Women in Castilian town society, 1100–1300*, Cambridge: Cambridge University Press. [3]

Duffy, Eamon, 1997. *Saints and sinners. A history of the popes*, New Haven and London: Yale University Press. [1–10]

Duvernoy, Jean, 1978. *Le registre d'Inquisition de Jacques Fournier, évêque de Pamiers, 1318–1325*, three volumes, Paris and The Hague: Mouton. [2]

Edwards, John, [1988] 1991. *The Jews in Christian Europe, 1400–1700*, London: Routledge. [7]

Edwards, John, [1992] 1996. 'The beginnings of a scientific theory of race? Spain, 1450–1600', in *Actas del XVII Congreso Internacional de Ciencias Históricas (Madrid, 1990)*, Madrid, 1992, pp. 625–636 [reprinted in *Religion and society in Spain, c. 1492,* ch.VII]. [See below] [8]

Edwards, John, 1994. *The Jews in Western Europe, 1400–1600,* Manchester: Manchester University Press. [6, 7]

Edwards, John, [1987] 1996. 'Christian mission in the kingdom of Granada, 1492–1568', *Renaissance and Modern Studies,* 31, pp. 20–33 [reprinted in *Religion and society in Spain, c. 1492,* ch. XI, see below]. [6]

Edwards, John, [1988] 1996. 'Religious faith and doubt in late medieval Spain: Soria *circa* 1450–1500', in *Past and Present,* 120, pp. 3–25 [reprinted in *Religion and society in Spain, c. 1492,* ch. III, see below]. [5, 6]

Edwards, John, [1989] 1996. 'Religion, constitutionalism and the Inquisition in Teruel, 1484–5', in *God and Man in medieval Spain. Essays in honour of J.R.L. Highfield,* ed. Derek W. Lomax and David Mackenzie, Warminster: Aris and Phillips, pp. 129–147 [reprinted in *Religion and society in Spain, c. 1492,* ch. XIII, see below]. [4]

Edwards, John, [1994] 1996. 'The popes, the Inquisition and Jewish converts in Spain, 1440–1515', in *New frontiers in Hispanic and Luso-Brazilian scholarship. 'Como se fue el maestro': for Derek W. Lomax in memoriam,* ed. T.J. Dadson, R.J. Oakley and P.A. Odber de Baubeta, Lewiston, Queenston and Lampeter: The Edwin Mellen Press, pp. 71–86 [reprinted in *Religion and society in Spain, c. 1492,* ch.V, see below]. [4, 5]

Edwards, John, 1996 *Religion and society in Spain c. 1492,* Aldershot: Variorum. [4,5,6]

Edwards, John, [1996] 1997. 'Jews and conversos in the region of Soria and Almazán: departures and returns', in *Religion and society in Spain, c. 1492,* [see above], ch.VI, and in *The Jews and the expulsion of 1492,* ed. Moshe Lazar and Stephen Haliczer,

Lancaster, California: Labyrinthos, pp. 277–287. [6]

Elliott, J.H., 1968. *Europe divided, 1559–1598*, London and Glasgow: Collins. [7]

Elliott, J.H., 1986. *The Count-Duke of Olivares. The statesman in an age of decline*, New Haven and London: Yale University Press. [8]

Estow, Clara, 1995. *Pedro the Cruel of Castile, 1350–1369*, Leiden: E.J. Brill. [3]

Eymerich, Nicolau, 1973. *Le manuel de l'Inquisiteur*, ed. and trans. Louis Sala-Molins, Paris: Mouton. [4, 5]

Fita, Fidel, 1887. 'La verdad sobre el martirio del Santo Niño de La Guardia, o sea el proceso y quema (16 noviembre 1491) del judío Juce Franco en Ávila', in *Boletín de la Real Academia de la Historia*, 11, pp. 7–134. [6]

Fita, Fidel, 1893. 'Concilios españoles inéditos: provincial de Braga de 1261, y nacional de Sevilla de 1478', in *Boletín de la Real Academia de la Historia*, 22, pp. 212–257. [4]

Fletcher, Richard, 1997. *The conversion of Europe. From paganism to Christianity, 371 –1386 AD*, London: Harper Collins Publishers. [1]

Fort i Cogul, Eufemia, 1973. *Catalunya i la Inquisició*, Barcelona: Editorial Aedos. [2]

Gampel, Benjamin R., 1989. *The last Jews on Iberian soil. Navarrese Jewry, 1479–1498*, Berkeley, Los Angeles, Oxford: University of California Press. [6, 7]

García Cárcel, Ricardo, [1992] 1998. *La Leyenda Negra. Historia y opinión*, Madrid: Alianza Editorial. [10]

Gracia Boix, Rafael, 1982. *Colección de documentos para la historia de la Inquisición de Córdoba*, Córdoba: Monte de Piedad y Caja de Ahorros de Córdoba. [4, 9]

Gracia Boix, Rafael, 1983. *Autos de fe y causas de la Inquisición de Córdoba*, Córdoba: Excelentísima Diputación Provincial. [5]

Greenleaf, Richard E., 1969. *The Mexican Inquisition of the sixteenth century*, Albuquerque: University of New Mexico Press. [7]

Griffiths, Nicholas, 1996. *The cross and the serpent. Religious repression and resurgence in colonial Peru*, Norman and London: University of Oklahoma Press. [7]

Gui, Bernard, 1964. *Manuel de l'Inquisiteur*, two vols, ed. and trans. G. Mollat, Paris: Société d'Éditions 'Les Belles Lettres'. [4, 5]

Haliczer, Stephen, 1990. *Inquisition and society in the kingdom of Valencia, 1478–1834*, Berkeley, Los Angeles, Oxford: University of California Press. [5, 6, 8, 9]

Haliczer, Stephen, 1991. 'The Jew as witch: displaced aggression and the myth of the Santo Niño de La Guardia', in *Cultural encounters. The impact of the inquisition in Spain and the New World*, pp. 146–156. [See Perry and Cruz] [6]

Hamilton, Bernard, 1974. *The Albigensian crusade*, London: The Historical Association. [2]

Hamilton, Bernard, 1981. *The medieval Inquisition*, London: Edward Arnold. [2]

Hamilton, Bernard, 1994. 'Wisdom from the East: the reception by the Cathars of Eastern dualist texts', in *Heresy and literacy, 1000–1350*, pp. 38–60. [See Biller and Hudson] [2]

Harvey, A.E., 1985. 'Forty strokes save one: social aspects of Judaising and apostasy', in *Alternative approaches to New Testament study*', ed. A.E. Harvey, London: SPCK, pp. 79–96. [1]

Hordes, Stanley M., 1991. 'The Inquisition and the crypto-Jewish community in colonial New Spain and New Mexico', in *Cultural encounters. The impact of the Inquisition in Spain and the New World*, pp. 207–217. [See Perry and Cruz] [7]

Inquisición y conversos. III Curso de Cultura Hispano-judía y Sefardí, Toledo: Asociación de Amigos del Museo Sefardí and Caja de Castilla-La Mancha. [4, 5]

Iogna Prat, Dominique, 1998. 'L'argumentation défensive: de la polémique grégorienne au "Contra Petrobusianos" de Pierre le Vénérable', in *Inventer l'hérésie? Discours, polémiques et pouvoirs avant l'Inquisition*', pp.87–118. [See Zerner] [1]

Jacobus de Voragine, 1993. *The Golden Legend. Readings on the saints*, trans. William Granger Ryan, Princeton: Princeton University Press. [2]

Jiménez Monteserín, Miguel, 1994. 'El auto de fe de la Inquisición española', in *Inquisición y conversos*, pp. 203–223. [See *Inquisición y conversos*] [4]

Kamen, Henry, 1988. 'The Mediterranean and the expulsion of Spanish Jews in 1492', *Past and Present*, 119, pp. 30–55. [6]

Kamen, Henry, [1983] 1991. *Spain, 1469–1714. A society of conflict*, London and New York: Longman [7]

Kamen, Henry, 1993. *The Phoenix and the flame. Catalonia and the Counter Reformation*, New Haven and London: Yale University Press. [8]

Kamen, Henry, 1997. *The Spanish Inquisition. An historical revision*, London: Weidenfeld and Nicolson. [4, 5, 6, 8, 10]

Kelly, J.N.D., 1963. *The pastoral Epistles. I and II Timothy, Titus*, London: A.&C. Black. [1]

Kermode, Frank, 1989. 'The Canon', in *The literary guide to the Bible*, ed. Robert Alter and Frank Kermode, London: Fontana Press, pp. 600–610. [1]

Klor de Alva, Jorge, 1991. 'Colonising souls. The failure of the Indian Inquisition and the rise of penitential discipline', in *Cultural encounters. The impact of the Inquisition in Spain and the New World*, pp. 3–22. [See Perry and Cruz] [7]

Ladero Quesada, Miguel Ángel, 1978. *España en 1492*, Madrid: Editorial Hernando. [4]

Lea, Henry Charles, [1889] [1890] 1967. 'El Santo Niño de La Guardia', in *Chapters from the religious history of Spain connected with the Inquisition*, New York: Burt Franklin, pp. 437–468. [6]

Lea, Henry Charles, 1906–1907. *A history of the Inquisition of Spain*, four volumes, New York: The Macmillan Company. [4–9]

Lea, Henry Charles, [1908–1911] 1963. *The Inquisition of the Middle Ages: its organisation and operation*, London: Eyre and Spottiswoode. [One-volume abridgement of the original three-volume edition] [2]

Le Roy Ladurie, Emmanuel, 1980. *Montaillou. Cathars and Catholics in a French village, 1294–1324*, Harmondsworth: Penguin Books. [2]

Llorca, Bernardino, 1949. *Bulario pontificio de la Inquisición española en su período constitucional*, Rome: Gregorian University. [4]

Lumia, Isidoro La, 1992. *Histoire de l'expulsion des Juifs de Sicile, 1492*, Paris: Éditions Allia. [7]

Luzzati, Michele, 1994. *L'Inquisizione e gli ebrei in Italia*, Rome and Bari: Laterza. [7]

Lynch, John, 1989. *Bourbon Spain, 1700–1808*, Oxford: Blackwell. [8, 9]

Martí Gilabert, Francisco, 1975. *La abolición de la Inquisición en España*, Pamplona: Ediciones Universidad de Navarra. [9]

Martínez Millán, José, 1984. *La hacienda de la Inquisición (1478–1700)*, Madrid: Consejo Superior de Investigaciones Científicas. [5]

Merlo, Grado, 1977. *Eretici e inquisitori nella società piemontese del Trecento*, Turin: Claudiana. [2]

Meyerson, Mark D., 1991. *The Muslims of Valencia in the age of Fernando and Isabel. Between coexistence and Crusade*, Berkeley, Los Angeles, Oxford: University of California Press. [6]

Monter, William, 1990. *Frontiers of heresy. The Spanish Inquisition from the Basque lands to Sicily*, Cambridge: Cambridge University Press. [6, 7, 8]

Moore, R.I., 1975. *The birth of popular heresy* [=*Documents of medieval history*, I], London: Edward Arnold. [1,2]

Moore, R.I., [1977] 1985. *The origins of European dissent*, Oxford: Blackwell. [1]

Moore, R.I., 1994. 'Literacy and the making of heresy, c.1000–c.1150', in *Heresy and literacy, 1000–1530*, pp. 19–37. [See Biller and Hudson] [1]

Moreno de los Arcos, Roberto, 1991. 'New Spain's Inquisition for Indians from the sixteenth to the nineteenth century', in *Cultural encounters. The impact of the Inquisition in Spain and the New World*, pp. 23–36. [See Perry and Cruz] [7]

Morrison, Karl F., 1992. *Understanding conversion*, Charlottesville: University Press of Virginia. [3]

Motís Dolader, Miguel Ángel, 1990. *La expulsión de los judíos del reino de Aragón*, two volumes, Saragossa: Diputación General de Aragon. [6]

Netanyahu, B[enzion], [1953, 1968, 1972] 1998. *Don Isaac Abravanel. Statesman and philosopher*, Ithaca and London: Cornell University Press. [6]

Netanyahu, B., 1995. *The origins of the Inquisition in fifteenth-century Spain*, New York: Random House. [5, 6]

Netanyahu, B., [1995] 1997. 'Sánchez-Albornoz' view of Jewish history in Spain', in *Toward the Inquisition. Essays on Jewish and converso history in late medieval Spain*, Ithaca and London: Cornell University Press. [5]

O'Callaghan, Joseph F., 1993. *The learned king. The reign of Alfonso X of Castile*, Philadelphia: University of Pennsylvania Press. [3]

Oxford Dictionary of the Christian Church, The, [1957] 1997, third edition, ed. F.L. Cross and E.A. Livingstone, Oxford: Oxford University Press. [1–10]

Perry, Mary Elizabeth, and Cruz, Anne J., (eds) 1991. *Cultural encounters. The impact of the Inquisition in Spain and the New World*, Berkeley, Los Angeles, Oxford: University of California Press. [6]

Peters, Edward, 1985. *Torture*, Oxford: Blackwell. [5]

Peters, Edward, [1988] 1989. *Inquisition*, Berkeley and Los Angeles: University of California Press. [9, 10]

Pimenta Ferro Tavares, Maria José, 1997. 'Expulsion or integration? The Portuguese Jewish problem', in *Crisis and creativity in the Sephardic world, 1391–1648*, ed. Benjamin R. Gampel, New York and Chichester: Columbia University Press, pp. 95–103. [7]

Porres Martín-Cieto, Julio, 1993. 'Visita guiada al Toledo de la Inquisición', in *Inquisición y conversos*, pp. 47–50. [See *Inquisición y conversos*] [5]

Prado Moura, Ángel de, 1996. *Las hogueras de la intolerancia. La actividad represora del tribunal inquisitorial de Valladolid (1700–1834)*, Valladolid, Junta de Castilla y León. [8, 9]

Pullan, Brian, 1983. *The Jews of Europe and the Inquisition of Venice, 1550–1670*, Oxford: Blackwell. [7]

Ratzinger, Joseph, Cardinal 1997. *Salt of the earth. The Church at the end of the Millennium. An interview with Peter Seewald*, trans. Adrian Walker, San Francisco: Ignatius Press. [10]

Reese, Thomas J., 1996. *Inside the Vatican. The politics and organisation of the Catholic Church*, Cambridge, Massachusetts: Harvard University Press. [10]

Renda, Francesco, 1993. *La fine del giudaismo siciliano*, Palermo: Sellerio Editore. [7]

Renda, Francesco, 1994. 'L'Inquisizione e gli ebrei in Sicilia', in *L'Inquisizione e gli ebrei in Italia*, pp. 121–160. [See Luzzati] [7]

Roth, Norman, 1995. *Conversion, Inquisition, and the expulsion of the Jews from Spain*, Madison: University of Wisconsin Press. [5, 6]

Rowland, Robert, 1994. 'L'Inquisizione portoghese e gli ebrei', in *L'Inquisizione e gli ebrei in Italia*, pp. 47–66. [See Luzzati] [7]

Rubellin, Michel, 1998. 'Au temps ou Valdès n'était pas hérétique: hypothèses sur le rôle de Valdès à Lyon (1170–1193)', in *Inventer l'hérésie? Discours polémiques et pouvoirs avant l'Inquisition*, pp. 193–218. [See Zerner] [2]

Sala-Molins, Louis, 1981. *Le dictionnaire des inquisiteurs*, Paris: Éditions Galilée. [5]

Sánchez Ortega, María Elena, 1988. *La Inquisición y los gitanos*, Madrid: Taurus [8]

Sayers, Jane, 1994. *Innocent III. Leader of Europe, 1198–1216*, London: Longman. [2]

Sicroff, Albert A., [1960] 1985. *Los estatutos de limpieza de sangre. Controversias entre los siglos XV y XVII*, Madrid: Taurus. [8]

Tanner, Norman P., (ed.) 1977. *Heresy trials in the diocese of Norwich, 1428–31*, London: Royal Historical Society. [2]

Tellechea Idígoras, J. Ignacio, 1977. *Fray Bartolomé Carranza y el cardenal Pole. Un navarro en la restauración católica de Inglaterra (1554–1558)*, Pamplona: Diputación Foral de Navarra. [7]

Thompson, Colin P., 1988. *The strife of tongues. Fray Luis de León and the Golden Age of Spain*, Cambridge: Cambridge University Press. [6]

Wakefield, Walter L., and Evans, Austin P. *Heresies of the High Middle Ages*, New York: Columbia University Press. [1, 2]

Weiss, Jean-Pierre, 1998. 'La méthode polémique d'Augustin dans le "Contre-Faustum", in *Inventer l'hérésie? Discours polémiques et pouvoirs avant l'Inquisition*, pp. 15–38. [See Zerner] [1]

Wigoder, Geoffrey, 1988. *Jewish-Christian relations since the Second World War*, Manchester: Manchester University Press. [10]

Zerner, Monique (ed.), 1998. *Inventer l'hérésie? Discours polémiques et pouvoirs avant l'Inquisition*, Nice: 'Z' Éditions. [1, 2]

INDEX